P9-DDX-294

From Call to Service
The Making of a Minister

FROM CALL
TO SERVICE

The Making of a Minister

by

Glenn E. Whitlock

The Westminster Press
Philadelphia

COPYRIGHT © MCMLXVIII THE WESTMINSTER PRESS

All rights reserved—no part of this book may
be reproduced in any form without permission in writing from the publisher, except by
a reviewer who wishes to quote brief passages
in connection with a review in magazine or
newspaper.

Scripture quotations from the Revised Standard Version of the Bible are copyright, 1946
and 1952, by the Division of Christian Education of the National Council of Churches,
and are used by permission.

LIBRARY OF CONGRESS CATALOG CARD No. 68–11214

Published by The Westminster Press ®
Philadelphia, Pennsylvania

PRINTED IN THE UNITED STATES OF AMERICA

To Emalee

Andrew L Taylor

16 June 72   1 67

45086

Contents

Foreword

WORKING WITH MINISTERIAL CANDIDATES during the past twelve
years has been a fascinating experience. My particular work
involves the psychological testing and counseling of candidates
required by the church prior to their ordination, and usually
preparatory to their entrance into theological school. They
have usually presented themselves for the required testing and
interviewing sometime during college, and they are counseled
up to the time of their graduation from the theological school
and their examination for ordination.

Since my work is also involved in recruiting men and
women for the church-directed ministry, my experience has
led me to conclude that the understanding of the ministerial
candidate and the recruitment for the ordained ministry are
interrelated. During the past few years, several denominational assemblies have made pronouncements about the problem of recruitment, but I have been struck with the paucity of
literature published about the "call to the ministry" and of any
discussion of the ministerial candidate himself. Since the
recruitment of ministerial candidates is the responsibility of
the entire church, this book attempts to provide a theological
and psychological framework within which the church can
fulfill its obligation to call out its members, and to provide the
necessary structure for the fulfillment of this ministry within
the community of believers.

Chapter III has been almost completely revised from "The

Call to the Ministry in the Reformed Tradition," in *Theology Today*, October, 1960. Portions of Chapters VI and VII, which have been completely rewritten, appeared originally in "The Choice of the Ministry as an Active or Passive Decision," in *Pastoral Psychology*, March, 1961, and in "Role and Self-concepts in the Choice of the Ministry as a Vocation," in *Journal of Pastoral Care*, Winter, 1963. Chapter IX has been almost completely rewritten from a lecture given at the "Seminar on the Ministry" at Columbus, Ohio, in 1963, sponsored by the Department of the Ministry, National Council of Churches. Portions of Chapter X, which have been reworked, appeared originally in "The Role of the Minister in Vocational Guidance," in *Pastoral Psychology*, September, 1961.

Reference is made to both men and women in the church-directed ministry throughout this book. However, the conclusions about ministerial candidates were limited to men. This limitation was made necessary simply by a lack of data available on women candidates. Now that there are increasing numbers of women ministerial candidates, a study will need to be made of them and of the factors surrounding their "call to the ministry."

Finally, I want to express my gratitude to persons who have made it possible to work with ministerial candidates. First of all, there are the candidates themselves, who have trusted me with their inner worlds. The Division of Vocation and Ministry of the Board of Christian Education and the Presbytery of Los Angeles of The United Presbyterian Church U.S.A. have made it financially possible to do a work that has given me a renewed sense of ministry. Susan Hubler, family and personal friend, has typed the manuscript and his given generously of her time to this project. Janice Keller, colleague and secretary, has been a thoughtful and helpful friend. Elliott and Carole have given meaning to parenthood and the time to write. My wife, Emalee, has given me both joy and an awareness that there are more important things in life than writing books.

                                                      G. E. W.

I

Introduction

THIS BOOK IS ABOUT MINISTERIAL CANDIDATES, the theological
dimensions within which they are called, their families and
social backgrounds, their personalities and motivations, and
the decision-making in which they choose to prepare themselves to serve in a particular ministry within the church. In
such a preoccupation with the ministerial student, there is no
intention of seeking to develop any uniform role expectations
of the ordained ministry. Indeed, it is not a matter of role at
all. It is simply a matter of examining the ways in which a
person's discipleship and selfhood may be actualized in a particular ministry. This work represents an effort to learn as
much as possible about these candidates who are challenged
by the community of believers to prepare themselves for the
ordained ministry.

The theological position regarding the ministry of the church
is presented more fully in the next two chapters, but in essence
it is that all Christians are called to a ministry, and some are
called to the ordained ministry to fulfill particular functions
within the community of believers. This book focuses upon
the ordained ministry, but not in any narcissistic preoccupation
with it to the exclusion of the ministry of all the people of God.
The complex nature of the function of this particular ministry
involves a professional dimension, which necessitates careful
study.

The professional has been described as a person who can do a good job even when he doesn't feel like it, because he has "learned his stuff." The ministry directed by the church is not a profession that is devoid of the personal dimension. The professional who "plays a role" or "acts a part" is not authentic as a person and hence is not a true professional. The professional dimension of the ministry is personal. It is a profession that is involved in meeting the needs of persons. It is professional in that the minister is ordained to serve people with a sense of objectivity which will prevent distortions in his own life from hindering his ministry to them.

This ministry directed by the church is also professional in the sense of requiring training to use certain tools. It involves training in the understanding of theology as the science of God, related to the concrete needs of persons. It involves the exploration of ultimate concern in relationship to the penultimate. Penultimate refers to "things before the last thing," or the preparation for the ultimate word from God. The ordained minister is trained to work with persons in terms of the penultimate concerns of physical and emotional suffering, and of the use of the means of grace taught by the church. The pastor is trained to communicate the ways in which God comes to persons. The ultimate word may be spoken at any moment by any follower of Jesus Christ, but he will need training to interpret the ways in which God comes to men. The understanding of these ways involves the theological and pastoral preparation of the ministerial candidate for the work of ministry with persons.

In this book, the ordained ministry will be referred to as an occupation within the context of Christian vocation. The occupation is the actual work in which the minister is involved with its particular functional requirements. It involves the work of a penultimate nature as well as the responsibility to speak the ultimate word to man in terms of his deepest personal needs. It involves the training necessary to prepare persons through pastoral education and counseling for the coming of the ultimate word. It is a church-directed ministry in contradistinction to those ministries directed by the world. The term "church-directed ministry" has been introduced by Arnold B. Come in his *Agents of Reconciliation,* and it is used here to designate a particular form of ministry. Although the church may develop many different forms of ministry that may come under its direction, this book is primarily concerned with those persons preparing for the ordained ministry within the church which gathers together a particular community of believers for study, worship, and witness.

Introduction to Studies

The story of ministerial candidates is an interesting one. Working with them as a counselor for more than ten years has been a fascinating experience. In psychological testing, interviews, and counseling sessions, some hundreds of candidates have revealed a lot about themselves. They have talked about their families and church backgrounds, their curricular and extracurricular interests, their early occupational aspirations, and their "call to the ministry." They have expressed their convictions and their understanding of Christian discipleship in the world. They are, for the most part, young men who are sensitive to the needs of the world, and who express their desire to work in the ministry of the church to meet some of these needs. They respond to these needs as an expression of obedience to Jesus Christ.

The candidates have raised serious questions with both theological and psychological implications. Their theological questions have become the basis for a renewal of study of the church's doctrine about the "call to the ministry." The empirical data that they have brought to their interviews have become a source of psychological studies. They were administered tests to determine the direction of their occupational interests. Personality and temperament tests and the interviews have helped to define the structure of personality of

these ministerial candidates, i.e., what motivates them, what
needs they have, and how they satisfy them.

These candidates were often curious as to what a psychologist was up to in the interview and sometimes hostile. It is
always interesting for a person to talk about himself, but it
may also be a threatening experience. After all, they were tell-
ing something about themselves, and they may have told more
than they had intended to tell. In addition to all this, the
interviewer was taking notes on what they said.

The tests themselves often pose a threat. College students
usually know something about what to expect from such tests.
There may be an aura of scientific objectivity surrounding
them, and they may expect that psychometric tests may give
them answers to their occupational and personal problems.
However, the expectation of scientific objectivity also involves
a potential threat. They fear that the tests may tell something
about themselves that they are not yet prepared to make
known. The candidate's ambivalence is evident in the interview, and yet his feelings may be useful in terms of helping
him to understand himself. This will better enable him to
fulfill the occupational requirements of the church-directed
ministry. A letter written by a theological student, several
years after he had been interviewed, illustrates how the interview can become the means by which the candidate may be
helped to understand himself in terms of requirements of the
ministry as an occupation.

> You may not remember it, but you really made an impression
> on me during that initial interview of being taken under care,
> back in 1953. Believe me, after that I was ready to think twice
> about the ministry. The incident is not complete, though,
> unless I tell you that that interview has affected my entire
> outlook during these past years. . . . Believe me, it has taken
> a lot of "grit" to meet that challenge you gave me. Although
> the immediate battle is not over, I feel strong enough now to
> see it through.

Confronting the ministerial candidate with a careful examination of any "pat answers" in relation to the ministry as an

occupation may help him to understand himself in terms of the requirements of the work. Some candidates tend to have an idealized image of the church-directed ministry which needs to be examined realistically while they are involved in their preparatory work. These years of preparation include both college and theological courses of study. The understanding of the occupation of the ministry comes not only through theological studies, but through the participation in the work and worship of the church and in relationships with all those within the community of believers. The growth of the candidate in his understanding of ministry involves not only the faculties of theological schools, but also the pastors, officers, and teachers within his local church.

Gathering the Data

It is important to understand something about ministerial candidates. Gathering all available data on them may help the church to understand its candidates, and to help prepare them to fulfill the functional requirements of the ministry. Learning about its ministerial candidates may also help the people of God to fulfill their responsibility for the order of the ministry. The community of believers is responsible to call out the ministers from their midst to use their "gifts." Some of these ministries will be "ordered" or directed by the world, and others will be directed by the church. The understanding of its candidates may help the community of believers to become more aware of both the "gifts" required for the ministry as an occupation, and the responsibility to "call" young men and women with such "gifts" to fulfill their ministries within the church.

The conclusions stated in this book are related to the study of ministerial candidates selected at random during a period of three years of work with them. The candidates talked about themselves and described their perceptions of themselves through the psychological tests. The interviewer simply observed and studied these descriptions, along with the information gleaned from the interviews. Notes on the interviews were studied to discover as much as possible about the ministerial candidate as a person, and to discover the ways in which the testing and interviews might be helpful to the church in understanding him and in counseling with him.

Each of the chapters studies one particular dimension of the formative factors in the candidate's preparation for the ordained ministry. Part One examines theological dimensions of the "call to the ministry." The "call to the ministry" is one expression of Christian discipleship, but it has been developed within the church to fulfill particular responsibilities of the church's mission. Part Two explores the ministerial candidate himself, including family and social background, personality and motivation, and the actual decision-making processes in which the choice of the ministry is made. The understanding of candidates for the ministry should be helpful to the church in its responsibility to call out able young men and women to fulfill particular tasks needful to the fulfillment of the church's mission. Part Three delineates the structure within which the church-directed ministry is developed, the kind of person needed in such a ministry, and the nature of fulfillment of this ministry within the community of believers.

The making of a minister involves first of all a "call to the ministry," which is placed within the context of Christian vocation. While all Christians are called to a ministry, the people of God direct certain persons to exercise their "gifts" in a particular way. This office is Christ's gift to the church, and the church orders its ministry in the training of the people of God for *their* ministry in the world. The work of training and equipping is not a *higher* order of ministry, but it is *prior* to the ministry enacted in the world.

Strictly speaking, the conception of a "call to the ministry" is a theological interpretation of a variety of human experiences. The conception of a "call" from God for a particular work is a recurrent theme that runs throughout both the Old and New Testaments. In the discussion of the theological dimensions of the "call" in the Protestant tradition, it is clearly indicated that a man must be "called to the ministry." He must be able to fulfill the requirements of his vocation by having had an authentic Christian experience, and by having the moral, intellectual, and psychological qualifications to fulfill the functions of the ministry as an occupation. The same aspects of the "call to the ministry" are evident throughout the history of the Protestant churches and at the present time.

Since they spend their formative years within the family constellation, the examination of their family backgrounds is crucial to any understanding of ministerial candidates. Such familial factors as the stability of the family within the community and the parental acceptance of responsibility are formative factors in the candidates' lives. Examination of their home religious environments, and the degree of parental relationship with the home church, provide additional dimensions of understanding. The social descriptions of ministerial candidates give some idea of their socioeconomic background, the degree of social mobility of their families, and the value that they give to education. Their curricular, extracurricular, and academic interests provide additional facets of understanding.

Motivational factors in the choice of the church-directed ministry are examined from various perspectives. The psychological studies indicate both conscious and unconscious dimensions of motivation. Early occupational goals, the persons influential in occupational decision, and the development of the choice of the ministry are studied. In the attempt to discover any differences between ministerial candidates who persist in their occupational choices and those who do not, various comparisons were made that reflected on their motivations.

Since occupational choices are related to personality and self-concept, the personality of the ministerial candidate is examined in terms of the choice of this particular ministry. Studies of their personalities indicate the type of person who tends to choose this type of ministry. The occupational interests of ministerial candidates, and their self-perceptions, are studied in terms of the psychological requirements of the church-directed ministry.

The decision-making processes are examined from a theoretical perspective including an understanding of the theological factors and of the psychodynamics involved. The decision-making processes are studied in relationship to the factors that seem to influence them.

The structure of the ministry as an occupation involves the outlines within which it is performed. There are theological dimensions to the church-directed ministry that will need to be understood both by the community of believers and by the candidates being called out of their midst to serve in particular ways.

There are also particular occupational requirements that involve both the psychological and intellectual dimensions of the church-directed ministry. They are outlined and related to the way in which a ministerial candidate might prepare himself for his theological education.

Fulfillment of ministry involves the personal meaning with which the ministerial candidate takes up his particular work in the church. This meaning involves both his theological understanding of the nature and mission of the church, and the psychological dimensions of his selfhood.

II

The Call to Ministry as a Christian Vocation

IN THE PROTESTANT TRADITION the understanding of the ordained ministry is inevitably related to the study of the nature and mission of the church. Within this tradition the church-directed ministry is considered as Christ's gift to the church for the sake of good order. It is not a matter of mere expediency worked out for the welfare of a human institution; it is a gift from God. It is simply a part of the structure of the church, and the function of this ministry is an integral part of the body of Christ. While it would be inaccurate to say that the church could not conceivably continue for a period of time without this ministry, it would be equally misleading to assume that it could do without it. Since it is given by God for the sake of order, the ecclesiastical discipline of the ordained ministry is necessary to the mission of the church. While the body can exist for a time without an organ, its work is, at the same time, seriously hampered. Since the church is dependent upon the Head alone, it is not absolutely dependent upon the special organ of the ordained ministry. Nevertheless, without this organ, the mission of the church is seriously impaired. Indeed, as Geddes MacGregor indicates: "For the Church to be entirely without a ministry, even for a very brief time, would be an immense deprivation, and the Church could not be the Body of Christ were it not, in such unfortunate circumstances, to seek by every possible means to restore to itself the ministry of which it had been deprived."[1]

The ministry of all Christians is not merely a human activity apart from the ministry of Christ. A man's ministry is not to be identified with Christ's ministry, and yet, it is not altogether separate from it. The church-directed ministry is simply a functional dimension of Christ's ministry, and it is indispensable to the health and wholeness of the church.

Throughout history, Protestant churches have had a continuing concern for the adequacy of the ordained ministry. This ministry is the responsibility of all the people of God. All those called to be his people are engaged in mission in the world. Every Christian is employed in "full-time Christian service." The call to that ministry directed by the church is not a call that sets a person apart from his fellows. It is simply a call to serve in a particular way. It is a call to do a particular task. It is a call by the church to a person to use his "gifts" of ministry in a special task.

The office of the ordained minister is properly placed within the context of Christian vocation. It is not an office that sets a man apart in terms of status. It sets him apart only in functional or operational terms. "Operational" is derived from *operari*, "to work." It is the special *work* of ministry to which a person is called. He is called to stand in the place where he can serve.

Robert Clyde Johnson has called attention to the use of "order" in reference to the ministry in the church. He points out that the word "order" (*taxis*) is from *tassō*, a term originally used in military parlance for the arranging or ordering of troops in preparation for battle. "When the word 'order' is applied to the Church, it should be understood first of all as a verb and only derivatively as a noun. Order in the Church *is* ministry, service, work. It is more of the nature of becoming than of being; more of the nature of a task than of a legacy."[2]

The office of the ordained minister is, then, *ordered* to fulfill certain tasks. Persons are called through the church to use their "gifts" in the way in which they are able to do their work of ministry. The mission of the church is given by God; but discipleship in the fulfillment of this mission is, or should be, ordered by the church. The ministry is Christ's gift to the church for the sake of good order; but the church must do the ordering. God *calls* a man to discipleship; but the church determines the *form* of his discipleship.

It is the responsibility of the church to build up itself for its mission. Perhaps it is more precise to say that it is involved in mission as the people of God are prepared for their ministry. The church does not exist for itself, but for its mission. It is involved in mission both in its church-directed ministry of "equipping the saints," and in its ministry of the people of God in their world-directed ministries. The different functions of the ministry within the church and the ministry in the world are equal in importance, but they are not the same in *form*. The work of the church-directed ministry is first only chronologically. The ministry of training precedes the ministry of the community of believers in the world. The task of "equipping the saints" is not a *higher* order of ministry, but it is *prior*. The theological training of the laity must precede their ministry in the world. If the church-directed ministry of preparation is not faithfully fulfilled, the ministry in the world will lack wholeness, vitality, and relevance.

Within the responsibility of "equipping the saints," the church-directed ministry is involved not only in the ministry of Word and Sacrament to the community of believers, it is also involved in the work of education and counseling that serves to prepare persons for the ultimate word. It is a ministry that proclaims the ultimate word to man, but it is also a penultimate ministry. The penultimate word is the next to the last word, which is the word that prepares the way for the divine-human encounter. This word of preparation may be communicated through all the relationships in which the pastor is involved in his educational and counseling ministry. Hence, ministers are ordained by the church to fulfill particular functional needs. They need to be able to meet these occupational requirements, and to receive the necessary training for their specialized work which consists largely of a penultimate form of ministry.

In terms of this understanding of ministry, the church's responsibility in the "call to the ministry" needs to be emphasized. If it is the church that does the ordering of the work of the ordained ministry, care needs to be taken both in understanding the "call" and in accepting the responsibilities related to the "call." The General Assembly of the Presbyterian Church in 1839 recorded these timely words: "The General Assembly feels it to be of unspeakable importance that weak, ignorant, and imprudent men should not be introduced into the ministry. Such men, though incapable of doing much good even if pious, yet may do immense mischief to the cause of religion, and only serve to bring the holy ministry into contempt, a result against which we are repeatedly admonished in the scriptures. It is not enough to increase the number of the clergy. The church's wants cannot be supplied by merely multiplying the number of ministers unless they are well qualified for the duties of the sacred office. Indeed, the greater the number of unsound, ignorant ministers, the greater the injury to the church." Other Protestant denominations have been similarly concerned.

With this sensitivity to the responsibilities of the ordained ministry, the understanding of the "call to the ministry" cannot be limited solely to any individual concern. There are various aspects of this "call" which must be considered together. A contemporary formulation of the various aspects of the "call" has been developed in a study of H. Richard Niebuhr as the result of work with The Study of Theological Education in the United States and Canada. The "call to be a Christian" constitutes the first aspect of the choice of the ministry as an occupation. Secondly, the "secret call" is that experience in which the person makes his occupational choice. Thirdly, the "providential call" includes the intellectual, psychological, and moral qualifications of the individual that indicate the necessary abilities for the work of the ministry. Finally, the "ecclesiastical call" indicates the invitation extended to the ministerial candidate to serve as a pastor to a particular congregation, and his subsequent election to ordination as minister of the Gospel.[3]

These four aspects of the call must be conceived as an integral whole. They are simply different dimensions of the call. The absence of any of the four parts means that the "call" is not complete. In any examination of this understanding of "call," a search needs to be made within the different denominational traditions for the particular theological understanding within that tradition.

The concept of the "secret call" needs some further elaboration. Traditionally, it has referred to the way persons respond to what they feel is a "call" to the ordained ministry. Such response is often interpreted as a "higher call" than to any of the other occupations. This confusing notion continues to be perpetrated on the Christian community by well-meaning teachers and preachers. In a book selected by a pastor's book club, the late Andrew Blackwood, a teacher of preaching and author of numerous books for pastors, insists that the calling of an ordained minister "ought to be *holier*" than the call to any other work. The religious environment of some congregations encourages the attitude that if a person is to be a "really committed" Christian, he will become an ordained minister. Ministerial candidates very often express their feelings that their "call to the ministry" is one which they consider to be higher than any other. Such an attitude usually reflects a limited understanding of the theology of Christian vocation and of the church's ministry, and such an understanding may be dismissed as evidence of theological immaturity.

However, regardless of the limitation of such attitudes in some ministerial candidates, one cannot escape the impression that at least some of them may be saying something of significance about their "call to the ministry" when they refer to it as a "higher call" to discipleship. What they say in their interviews is meaningful to them and needs to be taken seriously. Some of these candidates spoke of their Christian experience and their decision to study for the church-directed ministry in much the same way; thus, it appeared that they were often speaking not simply about an occupational choice of the minis-

try, but about a discovery of a sense of vocation. This discovery
of the meaning of Christian vocation involves the candidate in
a search for new patterns of obedience. He is, then, perhaps
for the first time in his life, willing to respond to particular
claims upon his obedience to God. Becoming sensitive to such
new patterns of obedience, he may become aware of a new
understanding of the church's mission. Discovering this new
sense of mission, he responds to the call to serve in a particular
function in which he feels he can express his obedience. His
feeling of response to the call to become an ordained minister
as a "higher call" may, in reality, be an experience of a deeper
response of obedience. His sense of "secret call" is, at first, not
so much to the ministry as a particular occupation as it is a
response of obedience in vocation. His discipleship in vocation
takes on meaning for the first time because he has responded
to the call to serve in a particular way. Within this understanding of the doctrine of vocation, the Christian is not so much
"called" by God to the particular occupation of the church-
directed ministry, but to discipleship in vocation. The church
simply orders the *form* of a person's ministry once he has
responded to the call to be faithful.

III

The Call to the Ministry
in the Protestant Tradition

THE MINISTRY OF JESUS is the prototype for the church's ministry. It is not merely a human, though hallowed, activity apart from the ministry of Christ. It is not to be identified with his ministry, but it is not altogether separate from it. It is the continuation of a ministry of service, "even as the Son of man came not to be served but to serve" (Matt. 20:28). It is a ministry of service to others.

The New Testament meaning of ministry (*diakonia*) is the humble service of the servant. The "call to the ministry" is a call to service. Although this "call" usually refers to the church-directed ministry in particular, God's calling (*klēsis*) involved the calling of men out of the world to be his people (*laos*). The usual distinction between clergy and laity in contemporary usage did not exist in the New Testament church. The "call" of God comes to all men, and the one who responds becomes one of the *laos*, the people of God.

Although the "call" to a ministry comes to all the people of God, specific powers are given by God to particular persons whom he chooses. These powers are given to fulfill God's purposes and are "gifts" of his grace. G. Ernest Wright argues that "the Bible's view is that God rules in his community, primarily or first of all, by his charismatic gifts, given where and when he chooses."[4] "*Charisma*" basically means a gift. It is used to indicate the special gifts or personal endowments that may be used in the service of the church, or it may refer to the gifts of God's grace and forgiveness. At any rate, it refers to the free and undeserved gifts from God.

The Call to the Ministry in the New Testament

In the letter to the Ephesians, God's gift or call is set forth in the following way: "And his gifts were that some should be apostles, some prophets, some evangelists, some pastors and teachers, for the equipment of the saints, for the work of the ministry, for building up the body of Christ" (Eph. 4:11–12). The "gifts" refer to the "*charisma*" that qualified them for their particular work. It appears likely that the various types of service within the Christian community are enumerated in order to illustrate the different kinds of "gifts" which men are given by God. The only thing we can be certain about is that not all of the "gifts" of ministry are included in this list. At the time of the writing of Ephesians, there was no official ministry in the church. "Men were not formally appointed to given offices, but exercised them as a matter of course in virtue of the special endowments which they had received from the Spirit."[5]

The incident reported in The Acts of the Apostles shows the way the calling of an apostle was acknowledged. Following Judas' defection, the early Christian community set about to select someone to take his place. Peter spoke of this need to select someone to take Judas' place who would have the proper qualifications:

> "So one of the men who have accompanied us during all the time that the Lord Jesus went in and out among us, beginning from the baptism of John until the day when he was taken up from us—one of these men must become with us a witness to his resurrection." And they put forward two, Joseph called Barsabbas, who was surnamed Justus, and Matthias. And they prayed and said, "Lord, who knowest the hearts of all men, show which one of these two thou hast chosen to take the place in this ministry and apostleship from which Judas turned aside, to go to his own place." (Acts 1:21–25.)

This incident affirms that it is God who calls the apostle to his work. This report of the selection of Matthias may be intended to show that the church possessed the power both to provide for the organization and to demonstrate the continuance of the church. However, it is clear that this power comes from God, and that Matthias is chosen for this office by the early church. At the same time, Paul's letter to the Ephesian church asserts that the "gifts" which qualify a person for his work are given not only to apostles but also to prophets, evangelists, pastors, and teachers.

In one of Paul's letters to the Corinthians, he indicates that the various gifts are given by God:

> Now there are varieties of gifts, but the same Spirit; and there are varieties of service, but the same Lord; and there are varieties of working, but it is the same God who inspires them all in every one. To each is given the manifestation of the Spirit for the common good. To one is given through the Spirit the utterance of wisdom, and to another the utterance of knowledge according to the same Spirit, to another faith by the same Spirit, to another gifts of healing by the one Spirit, to another the working of miracles, to another prophecy, to another the ability to distinguish between spirits, to another various kinds of tongues, to another the interpretation of tongues. All these are inspired by one and the same Spirit, who apportions to each one individually as he wills. (I Cor. 12:4–11.)

All these gifts are given to man by God. These gifts are used within the body of Christ. Paul then points out the specific functions to which he has appointed subjects within the church:

> Now you are the body of Christ and individually members of it. And God has appointed in the church first apostles, second prophets, third teachers, then workers of miracles, then healers, helpers, administrators, speakers in various kinds of tongues. (I Cor. 12:27–28.)

The Biblical record includes the foundation for the concept that a man is "called" or "appointed" to the ministry by God himself. This ministry is Christ's gift to the church. It is a gift

30 FROM CALL TO SERVICE

from God for the sake of good order, but it is the church that does the ordering. Certain persons are called out of the community of believers to use their "gifts" of ministry to fulfill particular functions. These "gifts" are used by the church in preparation for mission. The function of the church-directed ministry is to "equip the saints" so that they can fulfill their ministry in the world.

The Call to the Ministry in Calvin and Luther

One of the Reformers, John Calvin, was convinced that the concept of the ministry is inseparable from any consideration of the doctrine of the church. He insisted that the ministry is used by God to declare his will to his people in the church:

> Nevertheless, because he does not dwell among us in visible presence . . . , we have said that he uses the ministry of men to declare openly his will to us by mouth, as a sort of delegated work, not by transferring to them his right and honor, but only that through their mouths he may do his own work—just as a workman uses a tool to do his work.[6]

Calvin is talking about the particular form of the church-directed ministry as a "delegated work." God uses this ministry to continue the work that he began. Calvin had a high regard for the church-directed ministry, and his understanding has continued to be influential in the Protestant and Reformed tradition. In reference to this ministry, he wrote:

> I have accordingly pointed out above that God often commended the dignity of the ministry by all possible marks of approval in order that it might be held among us in highest honor and esteem, even as the most excellent of all things. God testifies that, in raising up teachers for them, he bestows a singular benefit upon men when he bids the prophet exclaim, "Beautiful are the feet and blessed the coming of those who announce peace" [Isa. 52:7], and when he calls the apostles "the light of the world" and "the salt of the earth" [Matt. 5:13–14]. And this office could not be more splendidly adorned than when he said, "He who hears you hears me, and

he who rejects you rejects me" [Luke 10:16]. But no passage is clearer than that of Paul in the second letter to the Corinthians, where he, as if purposely, discusses this question. He therefore contends that there is nothing more notable or glorious in the church than the ministry of the gospel, since it is the administration of the Spirit and of righteousness and of eternal life.[7]

In his work on the nature of the church according to the Reformed tradition, Geddes MacGregor remarks about Calvin's concept of the church's ministry:

No ecclesiology has ever more exalted the ministry, under Christ, than does Calvin's. The ministry is entrusted to frail humanity; but Christ's power sustains the feeble instrument of His choosing. The ministry is a weak vessel; but the precious freight that the vessel carries caulks her cracks. In this vessel He has deposited the keys of the Kingdom.[8]

MacGregor's reference to the ministry is that of the church-directed ministry. Calvin has been accused of having exalted this ministry in a way not consistent with the Biblical understanding of the ministry of all the people of God. He seems to place the entire responsibility for both nurture and evangelism upon the ordained clergy. He appears to relegate the ministry of reconciliation exclusively to the clergy. Although he encouraged a greater participation by the laity in the work of the church, he did not have the understanding of the church's mission through the ministry of all the people of God.

Another one of the Reformers, Martin Luther, placed greater emphasis upon the ministry of all the people of God. He talks about the vocation of the Christian to minister to the neighbor. The ministry of reconciliation between persons belongs to all the people of God. Indeed, to Luther, the only way the love of Christ can become real is through the way a man serves his fellowman through his vocation. He often speaks of man as a fellow worker with God, even though this sense of cooperation belongs on earth and not in heaven. As a fellow worker with God, man is called to act in certain ways. As he fulfills God's commandments, he is a fellow worker with God. He fulfills what is commanded through his vocation. In this sense, his cooperation is pointed not toward God, but toward one's neighbor.

Within his understanding of the ministry and mission of the church, Luther wrote in "The Babylonian Captivity of the Church": "As many of us as have been baptised are all priests without distinction. . . . Therefore we are all priests, as many of us as are Christians."[9] Hence, baptism was the basis for all men's ministry, and the "priesthood of all believers" became a fundamental tenet of the Reformation. All men are called to a ministry, and no one is superior to another in this calling.

Calvin did not have a clearly defined treatment of the work of the church. He was primarily concerned with the *form* of the church as an institution. Limited to his own historical situation, he was involved in defining the church over against Roman Catholicism. He was attempting to include the essential elements of the formal organization of the church in order that the structure might be an authentic expression of the body of Christ. He appeared to be preoccupied with his insistence upon the unique function of the church-directed ministry.

Although Calvin appears to be preoccupied with one segment of the church's ministry, he held this office of the ministry in such high esteem that he insisted that no man has a right to choose this work without having first been "called" by God:

> Therefore, in order that noisy and troublesome men should not rashly take upon themselves to teach or to rule (which might otherwise happen), especial care was taken that no one should assume public office in the church without being called. Therefore, if a man were to be considered a true minister of the church, he must first have been duly called [Heb. 5:4], then he must respond to his calling, that is, he must undertake and carry out the tasks enjoined.[10]

Luther also believed that a person did not choose the ministry ordained by the church all by himself. It was an office that was given to him. Again, in "The Babylonian Captivity of the Church," he reiterated his concept of the "priesthood of all

believers," but to be held along with some selection of particular persons to fulfill certain functions within the church:

> Let every one, therefore, who knows himself to be a Christian
> be assured of this, and apply it to himself,—that we are all
> priests, and there is no difference between us; that is to say,
> we have the same power in respect to the Word and all the
> sacraments. However, no one may make use of this power
> except by the consent of the community or by the call of a
> superior. For what is the common property of all, no individual
> may arrogate to himself, unless he be called.[11]

Both Luther and Calvin were careful to point out that men
should not take it upon themselves to seek the responsibilities
of the office of the ministry without having been called by God,
and having received the consent of the community of believers.
Both the calling of God and the consent of the people identify
the ministry as an office within the church. In "An Open Letter
to the Christian Nobility," Luther wrote:

> Priests, bishops or popes—are neither different from other
> Christians nor superior to them, except that they are charged
> with the administration of the Word of God and the sacra-
> ments, which is their work and office.[12]

He refers to this "office" of the ministry as "churchy" because
it grew out of the needs of the church as an institution and
was not founded in the Scriptures.

Hence, the ministry ordained by the church provides institutional order. Although it is "churchy," it is also necessary. In
discussing the order of the church, Luther defined his position
clearly in "On the Councils and the Churches":

> The Church is known outwardly by the fact that it consecrates
> or calls ministers, or has offices which they occupy. For we
> must have bishops, pastors, or preachers, to give, administer
> and use, publicly and privately, the four things, or precious
> possessions, that have been mentioned, for the sake of and in
> the name of the Church, or rather because of their institution
> by Christ. . . . The whole group cannot do these things, but

must commit them, or allow them to be committed, to someone. . . . This duty must be committed to one person, and he
alone must be allowed to preach, baptize, absolve, and administer the sacraments; all the rest must be content with this and
agree to it.[13]

Both of the Reformers were concerned about a person's
qualifications for the office of the ministry. Luther argued that
the most learned and pious members of the community of
believers should be elected to be the servant and guardian of
the Word and Sacraments, just as a mayor of a city is elected
on the basis of his qualifications for the office. "In a word, it
shall be a well-prepared, selected man."[14]

In terms of different aspects of the "call" to the ministry,
Calvin treated the subject under four headings. He discussed
who are to become ministers, how are they chosen, by whom
are they to be appointed, and by what rite or ceremony are
they ordained to their office. Calvin insists that the first creden-
tial of the ministerial candidate be that of his Christian experience. "To sum up, only those are to be chosen who are of sound
doctrine and of holy life."[15] This treatment includes the concept of the "call to be a Christian."

The concept of the "secret call" is included when Calvin refers to

that secret call, of which each minister is conscious before
God, and which does not have the Church as witness. But
there is the good witness of our heart that we receive the
proferred office not with ambition or avarice, not with any
other selfish desire, but with a sincere fear of God and desire
to build up the Church. That is indeed necessary for each one
of us (as I have said) if we would have our ministry approved
by God.[16]

Therefore, Calvin refers to the "secret call" whereby the individual declares his obedience in vocation and makes his choice
of the church-directed ministry. He discusses both the concepts
of the "call to be a Christian" and the "secret call" under the
subject of who are to become ministers.

The second subject includes the discussion of the way in

which ministers are appointed. Within this section Calvin discusses the care that must be taken to select men worthy of the office. He refers to Paul's admonition to Timothy not to choose anyone unworthy of the office. In this way, Calvin is discussing what has been referred to as the "providential call," which includes the intellectual, psychological, and moral equipment of the individual which indicate the "abilities" necessary for the work of the ministry. "Those whom the Lord has destined for such high office, he first supplies with the arms required to fulfill it, that they may not come empty-handed and unprepared."[17]

At one point, he is concerned that no man with a defect of character be chosen for the ministry who might destroy the authority of the ministry and bring disgrace upon the church. At another point, he writes concerning the responsibility of the church to the ministerial candidate: "We must always see to it that they be adequate and fit to bear the burden imposed upon them, that is, that they be instructed in those skills necessary for the discharge of their office."[18] Calvin referred to the responsibility of the church to examine men in regard to their qualifications to be chosen for the ministry:

> I refer the adverb "how" not to the ceremony of choosing, but to religious awe, which ought to be observed in the act of choosing. Hence, fasting and prayers, which Luke relates the believers used when they created presbyters [Acts 14:23, etc.]. For, since they understood that they were doing the most serious thing of all, they dared attempt nothing but with the highest reverence and care. But they especially applied themselves to prayers, in which they besought from God the Spirit of counsel and discretion [cf. Isa. 11:2].[19]

In reference to how the ministers are chosen, Calvin points out that the principle of the selection of the apostles cannot be used for the selection of the ministry. Nevertheless, he indicates that even in Paul's case, the church set him apart for his particular task. He referred to the passage in Acts. The Holy Spirit speaks to the apostles as they fast and pray: "Set apart for me Barnabas and Saul for the work to which I have called them" (Acts 13:2). Calvin points out that there would be no reason for the setting apart and laying on of hands after the Holy Spirit had attested their choice unless there was some ecclesiastical principle to be preserved. "God, then, could not approve this sort of order by a clearer example than, after having declared that he had appointed Paul apostle to the Gentiles, he nevertheless would have him designated by the church."[20] Hence, it is a responsibility required by ecclesiastical order that the church ordain a man to the ministry by the church. "We therefore hold that this call of a minister is lawful according to the Word of God, when those who seem fit are created [elected] by the consent and approval of the people."[21]

At the beginning of the Reformation, Luther had held that ministers should be ordained only in relation to a local congregation. According to Wilhelm Pauck:

> In Wittenberg and the electorate of Saxony, the method of calling and ordaining a minister remained fluid until about 1535. Until then the early teaching of Luther was followed according to which ordination was nothing else than the confirmation of the call to the ministry in a particular congregation. When a minister had received a call, he was examined on his fitness for the office. . . . If he was found to be qualified, he was elected and then, with prayer and the laying on of hands, commended to the congregation in its presence. . . .
>
> After 1535, ordination, still interpreted as *confirmatio vocationis,* became a separate ritual. As such it was now an act of the church government. . . . No candidate for the ministry could be thus ordained, unless he had been called and elected and until he had passed an examination. . . .[22]

The Call to the Ministry in the Evangelical Tradition

A similar concept of the "call to the ministry" is reflected generally in the Protestant churches as revealed in a study of the ministry in America from 1607 to the present. In a survey of the concept of the Protestant ministry from 1607 to 1850, Sidney E. Mead indicates that no major denomination made any "radical departure from the traditional view of Christians that the ministry is a vocation to which individuals are 'called'

of God."[23] He also points out that "basic piety" was a pre-
requisite to the ministry as an occupation. Since the function
of the minister was to proclaim the gospel, the Protestant
churches insisted that the minister be one who has already
accepted this gospel.

Mead points out five different factors on which all the evangelical Protestant churches placed some emphasis in regard
to the examination of the candidate for the ministry: "The
authenticity of his religious experience, the acceptability of his
moral character, the genuineness of his call, the correctness of
his doctrine, and the adequacy of his preparation."[24]

MacGregor calls attention to the fact that the Scottish church
preferred to leave hundreds of parishes without an ordained
minister than to ordain men who were not considered qualified
for the office of the ministry. In 1567 there were only 269
ministers in the Scottish church. In order to serve the additional congregations, there were 659 readers and other substitutes. "They recognized that they had to face, for the present,
a 'raritie of godlie and learned men', and make the best of the
situation."[25]

A survey of the Protestant ministry in America from 1850 to
the present points out the same tradition regarding the "call
to the ministry" as an occupation.

> It has been generally characteristic of evangelical Protestant-
> ism in America to single out a special call as fundamental.
> This call has been conceived as a summons from God made
> known to the individual through an identifiable and distinc-
> tive personal experience. It has been assumed that usually
> prior to this experience the individual has responded positively
> to a similar call to become a Christian.[26]

H. Richard Niebuhr, in collaboration with Daniel Day Williams and James Gustafson, has summarized the history of the
concept of the "call to the ministry" within the Protestant
churches.

> At no time have the Church and the churches not required
> of candidates for the ministry that they be first of all men of
> Christian conviction, however such conviction and its guaran-

tees were interpreted. The Church everywhere and always has expected its ministers to have a personal sense of vocation, forged in the solitariness of encounter with ultimate claims made upon them. It has also generally required that they show evidence of the fact that they have been chosen for the task by the divine bestowal upon them, through birth and experience, of the intellectual, moral, physical and psychological gifts necessary for the work of the ministry. Finally, in one form or another, it has required that they be summoned or invited or at least accepted by that part of the Church in which they undertake to serve.[27]

Summary

Strictly speaking, the conception of the "call to the ministry" is a theological interpretation of a variety of human experiences in their references to the "call to the ministry." The conception of a "call" from God for a particular work is a recurrent theme that runs throughout both the Old and New Testaments. Abraham is called to leave Ur of the Chaldees and to become the "father" of a people. Moses is called to lead the Israelites out of bondage in Egypt. Paul is called to be an apostle and a missionary to the Gentiles. In attempting to interpret their experience with God, the Biblical writers wrote of the "call" to particular responsibilities in the church and the world.

Luther outlined the basis for the office of the ministry. This office is to be considered no more important than any other office, but as he indicated in his "Sermons, 1544," "God gives you office that you may serve."[28] Whatever office is entrusted to you, you are called to exercise it faithfully. He also indicated that men were selected for this office out of the community of believers. It is from the most learned and pious of this community that persons are called to fulfill the particular functions assigned to the ministry directed by the church. Men are selected who can meet the qualifications for the office. However, even though the church ordains men to this particular office, only God will enable them to fulfill Christ's ministry.

Calvin attempted to understand and to interpret what the Biblical writers were saying. He developed a theology of the "call to the ministry." According to Calvin, the person "called" to the ministry must be able to fulfill the requirements of this office by having had an authentic Christian experience, by the development of a personal sense of vocation through a "secret call," by having the moral, intellectual, and psychological qualifications to fulfill the functions of the church-directed ministry, and by being elected to ordination to take up a particular work within the church.

He reflects the limited understanding of his historical period in reference to the ministry of all the people of God. In his development of the *form* of the church as an institution, he tends to center the ministry of the entire church in the clergy. He is primarily concerned with the calling and the "setting apart" of the ordained minister. Although he seems to interpret the "gifts" of the Holy Spirit as offices rather than functions to be fulfilled by all the people of God, he frequently refers to the functions or the occupational demands of the ministry that must be fulfilled by those persons responding to God's call. Having acknowledged his historical limitations and his preoccupation with the *form* of the church as an institution, Calvin nevertheless recognized the importance of the functional demands of the church-directed ministry, and the church's responsibility to the consent and approval of the "call." A similar attitude toward the "call to the ministry" is reflected in the history of the Protestant churches in America from 1607 to the present.

In order to understand the nature of the church in the Protestant tradition, it is necessary to examine the concept of the ministry. An understanding of the place of the ministry is integral to any formulation of the function of the church in the world or to any examination of the ministry of all the people of God. Any treatment of the concept of the ministry includes the study of the "call" to the particular tasks within the church, and the "gifts" or charisma of God to fulfill these tasks.

IV

Family Background and Social Descriptions of Ministerial Candidates

SINCE THE "CALL TO THE MINISTRY" comes through the church, the people of God need to know something about the ministerial candidate himself. The theological foundation for the church-directed ministry needs to be studied by pastors, officers, and teachers, but there is still a tendency within the church to think of the candidate for the ministry as some sort of unique person. It should be helpful to the entire community of believers to learn something about some representative candidates, and to understand more about the influences upon their lives.

The formative years of any person are spent within the family constellation. A person's background has to do with what he becomes. What happens, or what does not happen, in the home, influences the person in countless subtle ways. In terms of the background of a representative sample of sixty ministerial candidates from one denomination in the Protestant tradition, they usually come from the middle class and tend to come from families that are established in the community. Their families also tend to be stable in other ways. Only about 12 percent of these candidates came from homes that were separated by death or divorce. Nearly all the subjects from such homes had been enabled to work through their problems to the extent that they were attempting to understand and accept the meaning of the separated home. Since the children of divorced parents usually go with the mother, it was usually the father who was missing from the family constellation. It was not out of ordinary for the candidate's pastor to serve as a father surrogate, and these experiences were generally perceived as healthy ones by the candidates. Such a relationship with his pastor often had a decisive influence both upon his Christian experience and upon his occupational decision.

Although the largest percentage of the ministerial candidates expressed some degree of identification with, and acceptance of, parents as models for their lives, the percentage of parental rejection was relatively high. Some studies have indicated that low parental identification scores are associated with a tendency toward abnormality. However, in her *Values in Psychotherapy*, Charlotte Buhler questions the validity of such conclusions. She argues that if such a conclusion is valid, a great number of our young adults would have to be abnormal. She points out that adolescents and young adults in the decade of the sixties are groping for some sense of identity, but parents are often the farthest from their minds when it comes to looking for models to emulate.

Home Religious Environment

Evaluation of the candidates' written statements about the religious environment in their homes, and the interviewer's ratings of the degree of the parents' relationship to the church, provided the basis for several conclusions. Over 54 percent of the candidates indicated a religious environment in the home that was evaluated as Christian. The degree of religious practices, such as family devotions, varied within this group as evidenced in the various expressions regarding their home religious environments. Some of the typical comments were as follows: "My home environment has always been Christian. It was difficult for me to see where my home influence ended and where my own conviction began." "I was born in a Christian home and went to church almost all my life. Grace was always said at the table, and I was encouraged to read the Bible." "Our family was Christian and church-related. We practiced family devotions and participated in the work as well as the worship in the church. It was good and healthy for the most part."

In a somewhat different kind of response, one candidate wrote: "My home religious environment is a very provocative one. Not everyone in my family professes the same faith or belief, and yet we are very religious in that we all accept the same God. Not all my family accept Christ, but they are still religious. Because of this, the environment is very provocative as well as challenging in that we have different ideas on certain subjects to be discussed from different vantage points. I would say, with all sincerity, we have a Christian community for a religious environment."

Another candidate said: "Our home is religious in terms of love and unselfishness and respect for each other and God. We have always been members of the church, though in differing degrees of activity and responsibility (according to the social-economic situation of the local church of my parents at that time—we have moved a great deal). Grace has always been returned at every meal as long as I can remember. We pledge support to the church and attend regularly. We have just started, this year, to have a time of family devotions and Bible reading every night at dinner and find it invaluable. I have always been encouraged by my parents in my interest in a church vocation, but not 'pushed' in that direction." One candidate mentioned some of the specific aspects of their family religious rituals: "Active in weekly services, and in the general program of the church we were affiliated with or a member of. The immediate home environment was one in which personal religious devotions were assumed. Collective family worship in home at mealtimes and on festive occasions of the year were held around the piano. There was quite a bit of musical talent in my parents and brother. Parents tended not to initiate Bible study in the home, but relied on church programs to instill

Biblical lore. Christian attitudes and principles, however, were taught in the home."

Another 9 percent of the candidates indicated that at least one of the parents was Christian, and that they received religious training in the home at least through that one parent. Some of the typical comments were as follows: "My mother, sister, and two brothers are Christians, my father is not. We have worship and counsel together as a family about spiritual things, but without my father." "My mother is a Christian and a member of the church. She has always tried to live a Christian life. My father is not a Christian, but I hope he will come to Christ in the near future. He believes, but has failed to make that first step."

A somewhat different kind of comment indicated that although both parents were members of the church, only the mother provided some degree of religious support. "All members of my family are members of the Presbyterian church, but the church has not figured prominently in our home life. Only my mother and I attend church. My mother has a strong personal faith. My father has not. Until the time of my Christian decision, 'religion' had had no real bearing on my home environment."

About 37 percent of the candidates indicated varying degrees of a lack of religious training or support in the home. Types of home environment varied from acknowledgment of the church and the Christian faith to actual opposition. Some comments acknowledged the moral qualities of the parents: "Mother and Father are strong morally. They get along well using a Christian philosophy in living. Religion was almost never discussed at home. Moral righteousness was emphasized." "Our home is strong in the ethical and moral tradition of Christianity, but weak in the real cause and starting point of such a tradition. We attended church only spasmodically as a family, only on Easter and Christmas."

Others mentioned that their parents were nominal Christians, but with no evidence of any Christian influence in the home: "I do not have much of a religious environment, and all my Christian thought has been derived from the church. My parents are good people and my father goes to church, but there is no direct Christian influence in my home." "As a child, we attended church rather irregularly. My parents are nominal Christians, but no longer attend church. We had no religious instruction at home, except for grace at meals."

Some parents, though not members of any church, were sympathetic to the values and commitments of the candidate: "My parents are increasingly in sympathy with my religious outlooks, but they are not themselves members of any church." The curt remark of one candidate was revealingly indicative of his parents' attitudes: "Neither parent is Christian. They are both agnostic."

In evaluating the degree of activity of parents in the life of the church, we find that candidates for the ministry tend to come from homes where parents are active in participation in the work and worship of the church. However, there are a number of candidates who come from homes where participation in the life of the church is minimal.

Social Descriptions

Knowing something about the social description of these subjects may help toward understanding ministerial candidates. One of the ways to learn about the social definition of a person is to discover his father's occupation, which is probably the best single indicator of the social and economic status of the family. A check on the occupation of the candidates' fathers showed that only 10 percent of the sixty candidates came from the professional or teaching occupations, and only one of these was a minister. Over 51 percent of the candidates' fathers were employed in various businesses, including management, sales, office work, and self-employed owners. The remainder of the fathers' occupations were distributed between engineering, skilled and unskilled labor, agriculture, and governmental administrative positions. Such evidence points to the tendency toward upward social mobility with those who have chosen the ministry as an occupation.

Over 81 percent of the candidates rejected their father's occupation as being one that would not interest or challenge them. This rejection may be variously interpreted. It could mean the rejection of the father himself, or of the father's values. However, it may simply reflect the autonomous voice of the candidate's own interest, rather than that of his parents. It may also reflect the father's rejection of his own occupation, and his son's identification with this attitude as reflected in one instance where the candidate remarked, "My father really wanted to become a lawyer."

Another way in which a person says something about himself is the initiative that he takes in providing for his own college education. While some students do not need to provide financially for their college training, those who do so are expressing something about their motivation to reach their particular occupational goals. The extent to which a candidate works through any such obstacles helps to give both a social and a motivational description of the candidate. Over 63 percent indicated they were earning one half or more of their college expenses. Without exception, every candidate had some job outside school with which he paid for some of his expenses.

Curricular and Extracurricular Interests

In an examination of the extracurricular activities of the candidates while they were in college, their interests were divided into various types. There were organizational interests expressed through leadership in student government, sports, and social-relational interests that included persons active in organizations such as clubs and fraternal groups. There were those candidates who appeared to have a primary concern with church organizational participation, which included those whose specific interests were in organizational leadership, social relations, and what might be termed as religiously oriented service or values. There were candidates with interests in music or the performing arts. Interest primarily in scholarship indicated by membership in honorary scholastic fraternities was expressed by only 10 percent of the candidates. The predominant pattern of interests centered around the various types of social-relational interests that involve group and interpersonal concerns.

Although no specific pattern of interests or personality for ministerial candidates may be derived from such limited data, it is quite evident that the composite image of the minister in the Reformed tradition has changed from that of the scholarly preacher of past eras to the social-relational type of interests and leadership. The composite image of the academic interests of candidates shows an obvious emphasis upon the liberal arts. There was relatively little interest in academic studies outside the areas of history, philosophy, literature, and social sciences. The degree of interest in the social sciences, including psychology, sociology, and anthropology, may express a new direction of interests for ministerial candidates. The increasing importance of the pastoral role may be reflected in the degree of interest of ministerial students in the social sciences. Most of the candidates indicated that the reason for the choice of their academic majors was that such a study could be of help to the pastor in his work. Ministerial candidates are usually quite observant of their own pastors and are often sensitive to the ways in which their ministries might be strengthened. Hence, their choice of an academic major within the social sciences may be indicative of their understanding of their ministry as one of service to persons.

In terms of their academic ability to do graduate work in a theological school, the college grades of candidates give some indication of intellectual ability. The overall average of the subjects' grades was about a B minus. In their talking about how they felt about their classes, it was evident that most of the ministerial candidates have responded positively to their college courses. The largest percentage indicated they had experienced intellectual stimulation from their courses in college.

In reference to a consideration of grades, it is interesting to note the results of a study of a group of highly creative architects. They only showed a B average for their college grades. In the courses in which they were interested, they could earn top grades, but they were willing to do practically nothing in the courses that failed to interest them. They tended to be somewhat rebellious against the standards set by the educational institutions.[29] Now, it would be inaccurate to equate the conclusions regarding grades of creative persons in this study with the grade average of the ministerial candidates. Nevertheless, the theological schools of the church may be cautioned never to make the grade-point average the sole criterion of the potentiality of the ministerial candidate. It is interesting to note that one of the most creative architects in the study referred to was advised by the dean of his school to quit because he had no talent.

While it is impossible to give an accurate measure of the candidate's intellectual capacity, suffice it to say that the combination of ability and motivation expressed through grades do not give a picture of academic excellence. Such evidence is consistent with the direction indicated by their extracurricular interests. Neither scholarly interests nor academic excellence characterize the ministerial candidate in the contemporary church in the Protestant tradition. It is very likely that this state of affairs is largely the result of the attitude of those within the church in reference to what they consider to be really important in pastoral leadership. Hence, students with scholarly interests and superior academic capabilities are not ordinarily motivated to choose one of the church-directed ministries in which to express discipleship. To the degree that this conclusion is valid, the denominations within the Protestant tradition are in serious trouble. Despite the caution in reference to grade averages, the need for students with first-

rate intelligence and with aptitudes for theological thought is
of equal importance to any of the other requirements of the
pastorate, and equal in importance to standards set by any of
the other occupations or professions.

V

Motivations of Ministerial Candidates

WITHIN THE PROTESTANT TRADITION, persons refer to the "call to the ministry." The theological definition of the "call" is an interpretation of a variety of human experiences and is not to be interpreted as a fact but as a statement of meaning. The psychological study of motivation to choose the ministry as an occupation is not to be confused with the theological interpretation of the "call to the ministry." Nevertheless, psychologically, each person does make a decision or choice of an occupation, and the choice of the ministry is always a culmination of both conscious and unconscious processes.

Motivating factors involve both conscious and unconscious needs of ministerial candidates. Such needs may be illustrated by the strong drive of some persons to be liked and accepted by others. Such needs may also be expressed by the attitude of "I can't do enough for God." While such a statement may involve some basic theological truth, it is usually the expression of a basic need or insecurity that prompts a person to attempt to win God's acceptance through good works.

Another dimension of motivation is the choice of goals of life. In his *The Doctor and the Soul*, Viktor Frankl, a psychiatrist, has indicated that man is oriented toward a goal of potential meaning and values which may be actualized by him. From her research in child psychology, Charlotte Buhler has pointed out that a "task aspect" develops in the child at about four years of age. She feels that children seem to develop a task-

oriented attitude at this early age. It is an attitude that expresses a new type of motivation, and it seems to develop
following a child's first genuine goal-setting.[30]

Studies in Motivation

Studies of the various types of theological students in The
Study of Theological Education in the United States and
Canada included an evaluation of ten specific factors that lead
a student to choose the ministry as an occupation. These types
of experiences seem to be an adequate summary of the variety
of factors which appear to motivate candidates to choose the
ministry as an occupation:

(1) There is the student who is in seminary because his
parents, pastor, and home congregation have decided for him
that he will make a good minister. (2) A man may be suffering from deep wounds in himself and seek through theological
education to heal his own disturbed mind and spirit. (3) A
student who functions well in interpersonal relations and
anticipates the prestige and success that will be forthcoming
from a ministerial career will find his way to seminary. (4) A
person who has prematurely tasted the fruits of success in a
church career as a boy evangelist, dynamic youth leader,
or student movement executive must complete what are to
him often only *pro forma* requirements for ministerial status.
(5) The man who decided for the ministry at an early age,
frequently out of a sense of alienation in the world, and who
enjoyed the protection of the pre-ministerial group in college
will find his way to seminary. (6) A zealous spirit characterizes the student who has found a gospel and knows its saving
power. He wishes to share his good news with the world.
(7) Religion and theology present themselves as objective
intellectual problems to a searching mind, and a theological
school seems to be the place to pursue a study of these problems. (8) An experience of a tragically disorganized society, or
of disordered minds, often leads a student to study for the
ministry. He sees the church as an institution out of which
flow healing processes for the social and personal evils of our
time. (9) Frequently found in the present generation is a man
seeking for a faith adequate to bring order into the intellectual
and moral confusions that have characterized his previous per-

sonal and academic experience. (10) Finally, there is the rare student of mature faith who lives in the knowledge that it is God who saves and justifies. He is seeking to become an adequate servant of his Lord.[31]

Various studies of the unconscious factors influencing the choice of the ministry as an occupation have been made, and the discovery of these factors through psychological tests and interviews are helpful in counseling with candidates. However, despite immature influences upon an original decision, motives may change so that a mature motivation may develop which will be relevant to the actual occupational requirements of the ministry. Whatever the origin of the candidate's decision to become a minister, the process of his theological preparation and his work as a minister carries him far beyond the original motivating factors. His preparation for the work of the ministry and his experiences in this work may so alter his original motivations that the need and meanings originating the decision are seldom the same factors which motivate him to continue in the ministry. If the original immature motives persist, the person, of course, remains immature. However, if he is able to give himself to meet the occupational requirements of the church-directed ministry, these demands alter the original motives, and the individual is pushed to the "growing edge" of his own maturity. To the extent that he is able to understand himself through his experiences in his vocation as a Christian student during his years of preparation, the ministerial candidate is able to mature to the point where new motivations become evident. Every time reality is honestly faced in his response to the vocational demands of discipleship, the ministerial candidate gains an integrity that provides additional maturity of motivation for the ministry for which he is preparing.

The Development of the Occupational Decision

In terms of personal influences upon the candidate's decision, pastors were mentioned as the greatest single influence on their lives and upon their "call to the ministry." Parents were mentioned as a close second in influence, and mothers appear to wield a greater influence than fathers. The combined influences of the church and home were the crucial factors in most of their decisions. Knowledge of these crucial influences have implications for the Christian education program of the church in terms of the way in which the church helps a family to fulfill its unique ministry.

In addition, the persons who represented the most ideal qualities to the ministerial candidates were pastors and theologians. Over 60 percent of them mentioned their own pastors, university pastors or college chaplains, and nationally known preachers and theologians such as Paul Tillich, Reinhold Niebuhr, Billy Graham, and Peter Marshall. This stage of development, characterized by identification with other significant persons, is a part of the process of self-actualization. Encountering someone who represents an ideal of fulfillment in vocation on the contemporary scene may be the most important single event in the life of a ministerial candidate. The image of the ideal may be an integrating experience that enables the individual to make a decision that he would otherwise be unable to make.

Since preparation for the ministerial office is a highly personal experience, questions of religious doubts trouble ministerial candidates. It is important for the church to provide a permissive environment in which these questions may be honestly discussed. Forrest Youngquist, a pastor who had served the church for nearly fifteen years, announced to his congregation in a sermon in December, 1959, his sensitive reappraisal of his choice of the ministry as an occupation and his decision to leave the church-directed ministry. His statement is a sensitive evaluation of the developing process of his occupational decision.

One of the marks of maturity is the ability and the assumed responsibility of making choices, of determining within the limits possible for us what we shall or shall not do or be.

Without the liberty of relative self-determination of one's life, there can be little growth in being a more real person. Such self-determinism is the gracious liberty God gives us so that from the exercise of it we are more free to give ourselves over to his will.

But what if, in a tumultuous thirty-ninth year of life in which there has been more growth than in any other period of one's life, there comes a question, "What was the nature of the choice I made to become a minister?" In answer, it is clear to me now that it was based upon immature reasons not then realized or pointed out. The choice was then immediately acted upon and reacted to by people in such a way that continued liberty in the choice was taken away. It is not that the choice would have been reversed, but the choice would have been strengthened properly had it remained an open decision with the possibility of reversal while the life was still so immature in relationship to such a decision.

Now please remember and understand—this does not deny the validity of the call of God at that time through the immature experience of a sixteen-year-old boy, but that call should have been given time to ripen and be bolstered by more mature reasons before it was thought irrevocable. Instead, it was immediately acted upon and commitments made so that this sixteen- and seventeen-year-old felt guilty in even questioning his decision. Now, against the backdrop of a considerable degree of emotional immaturity that is finally struggling to grow, the factor of not having had continued liberty then to exercise choice for oneself has become exceedingly important. This is really the crux of the matter. There was not enough of the mature "me" in the decision. Even though the decision was right, yet it has remained on this immature footing. Now the maturing person wants to be responsible for his decisions. Granted the freedom at this time to choose whether or not to be a minister, would I so choose? This decision cannot be made from within the vocation itself. It is not an open question for one who has never known any other possibility. For me, developing selfhood involves becoming a more mature person—especially emotionally—which requires the making of a responsible choice for my life under God now.

This is what is back of a good deal of my dissatisfaction in the ministry during the past months. . . . This dissatisfaction stems not from disagreeable tasks—of which every vocation has some—but rather from the continuing question, "Is this what God wants me to do with my life now—in this period of growing selfhood?" I am a different person today than I was up to a year or two ago. The reasons for being in the ministry that were valid for that more immature person are no longer valid for the person I am now. A person, incidentally, whom God has graciously led into depths of spiritual understanding recently that have made the Christian life and the Scriptures to be new and vitally relevant.

Then at sixteen, God called me through the appeal of a man, and through the example of older friends who were entering the ministry. God worked even through the interested concern but unwise adulation of a church that thrust too young a boy too far ahead too soon. These and a number of other significant events and situations stunted the emotional development and brought a degree of unreality to the life. These have had serious inner repercussions as the years have gone by. They have finally forced this total reevaluation of life. They have brought the necessity of realizing my selfhood as a maturing person through the responsible remaking of some of life's choices where this possibility still exists.

The church needs to guard against any exploitation of its ministerial candidates, as is evidenced in this personal statement. Such exploitation in the form of "unwise adulation" or in the increasing involvement of the candidate in the organization of the church is usually done with the "best of intentions." Such candidates who are always involved in leadership roles are not free to explore their doubts. In many instances, teaching a church school class or sponsoring a junior high fellowship does not provide a candidate with the necessary freedom to understand himself in relationship with his peers, or with God. It was not a contemporary psychologist but John Calvin who insisted that without knowledge of self there is no knowledge of God. Each ministerial candidate deserves the opportunity to have some freedom from leadership responsibilities in order to become a real person.

It is the church's obligation to provide not "unwise adulation" but a relationship within which the ministerial candidate can honestly and fearlessly explore his doubts and his affirmations. The church needs to provide for such a nonthreatening relationship within the community of believers in which his maturing occurs and/or within some structure provided by the denomination. Counselors need to be made available both to pastors and ministerial candidates for the sake of developing selfhood. It is far more important to God and to the church that a candidate become a more real person than that he continue as a candidate for the church-directed ministry. It is the maturing self who has become the obedient disciple. God is surely more interested in discipleship than in any numerical additions to the ministerial office.

The Persistence of Occupational Goals

One approach to the understanding of the motivation of ministerial candidates is to examine the persistence of their childhood occupational aspirations. In tracing the interests of candidates from their early occupational goals, we found evidence of a steadily developing pattern of interests in the direction of the social service or helping occupations in which persons are involved in interpersonal relationships in the performance of their work. The types of occupational goals selected by students in their childhood show a remarkable degree of persistence. On the other hand, some students with childhood interests in the sciences, mechanics, and business made their choice of the ministry as an occupation sometime during college. These students evidenced a change of interest in such a choice, but a large percentage of these candidates dropped their occupational interests in the ministry and returned to their earlier interests before completing college. In contrast, there were very few dropouts among those whose childhood interests were centered in the social-service occupations. The choice of the ministry as an occupation was simply a continuation of their early pattern of interests and ideals in the area of work in which they could serve and help others. In her *Values in Psychotherapy,* Dr. Buhler points out that the early evidence of a motivational pattern regarding ideals seems to be developing at the age of four years. She indicates that these early motivational patterns of ideals are much more persistent than many later-conceived goals.

The way persons perceive themselves tells something about them and their motivation. In a comparison between the self-perceptions of ministerial candidates who persisted in their occupational goals and those who did not, there were some noticeable differences that may contribute to the understanding of the motives of the mature ministerial candidate. The comments of candidates who did not persist in their occupational goal have some interesting similarities. They tend to lack persistence in goal achievement. They perceive themselves as tending to procrastinate and lacking in personal discipline. There are comments such as: "I set goals and then frustrate myself by failing to carry through." "I am purposeful but what I don't like the most is my procrastination." "I am impatient with the lack of discipline in my personal life." "I don't like my laziness or procrastination or carelessness." "I lack discipline." They may be persons who get along easily with others but they seem to lack the ability to pursue their goals in a disciplined fashion. They may tend to be optimistic by nature, but they also tend to be unrealistic about what can be accomplished.

In addition, these candidates seem to show a more passive orientation and a tendency to become more involved in immediate rather than long-term goals. There were responses such as: "I need to be admired and loved." "I am moved by other people and influenced by others' thoughts." "I think that I am kind of weak and have a temptation to sin and lust." "I am weak in organization and getting things done." "I can't apply myself to my studies."

A random selection of the self-perceptions of the ministerial candidates who persisted in their goal achievement showed some demonstrable difference compared with those who did not. Although some of these candidates indicated an awareness of lack of persistence, it was not a noticeable pattern. These candidates tended to express themselves in relationship to persistence in goal achievement: "I am a thorough person." "I am not able to be as scholarly as some of my peers, but I have the perseverance and a creative imagination and empathy." "I feel that I am a determined person. I carry through with my ideas." These candidates seem to demonstrate a healthy acceptance of themselves. They tended to accept both their strengths and their weaknesses. Some of their responses show this acceptance of both the positive and negative feelings about themselves: "I feel that I am a person with a good deal of potential both intellectual and emotional, but I have too much pride." "I feel I have a good personality." "I like it that I am able to grasp my studies easily and that I seem to be generally talented." "I enjoy the fact that I am able to understand and that I have the intellectual capacity."

In addition, these candidates appeared to be more oriented and involved in long-term rather than in immediate goals. Some of their responses demonstrate this orientation: "I am slow in learning but I am willing to make the effort to do what is needed to use what God has given me." "I have a terrific drive and I have the ability in analyzing problems." "I am active in leadership." "I like taking part in activities with people." "I want to get in and work." Such candidates seem to be more oriented toward the work of the ministry rather than being dependent upon the meeting of ego needs in immediate goals. Since the pastor rarely sees the immediate results of his work, he needs to be the kind of person who can tolerate work goals that are long-range and that cannot be immediately achieved. He needs to be the kind of person who can encounter frustration and temporary failure without adopting a defeatist attitude.

The study of motivation for the ministry as an occupation is complex. It may involve the inner needs of the individual to atone for his guilt, or to deal with his feelings in regard to his identity as a person. Motivation inevitably involves both the individual needs to be met and the goals that a person sets for his life in order to achieve some sense of self-actualization in the fulfillment of his ministry. The ministerial candidate's identification with some significant person may constitute a significant motivational factor. Theologically, the true image or symbol claims total surrender, and it is idolatory if this surrender is made to anything less than God. To the Christian, the true image of man is Jesus Christ, and it is his image around which integration of the personality of the ministerial candidate should be effected. The persistence of goals is related to the efficaciousness of the image or symbol on which the choice was made in the first place. If the personality surrender expressed through the decision of the candidate is limited or distorted, he will react in one of two ways. Either he will drop his plans to study for the ministry, or his motive will become fixated on a goal that is unhealthy both for the church that he is called to serve and for himself and his needs for self-actualization. If the motivation of the ministerial candidate is one of identification with Jesus Christ as the expression of man's true selfhood, such an identification provides for the integration of the whole person in relation to self-actualization and to meeting the requirements of the church-directed ministry.

VI

The Personality of the Ministerial Candidate

PERSONALITY AND OCCUPATIONAL choices are closely inter-related. Persons tend to choose occupations that are peculiarly important to them in relationship to their personality characteristics, and the ways in which they usually handle their problems. Integral to the consideration of personality is the person's self-concept. The self-concept is the way a person looks at himself. It includes his feelings, goals, ideals, hopes, and ambitions. It involves the way he looks at himself in relationship to anything he does. The way an individual looks at himself and understands himself is crucial to any choice of occupation. His choice of occupation is influenced largely by his self-concept. The self-concept is a major determinant in the choice of the ministry as an occupation, and such a choice is an implementation of the way a candidate looks at himself.

In the occupational choice of the ministry, self-understanding and self-acceptance are far more important than increasing the supply of occupational information. The way a person understands and accepts himself influences his occupational interests. Personality and interest tests reveal the individual's concept of himself, and his occupational interests will change as his self-concept changes. In this sense, occupational interests are dynamic phenomena that reflect the changes in the individual's perception of himself.

If occupational interest demonstrates an individual's under-

standing of himself, these interests must indicate something
about his personality and motivation. It is not simply an indication of interest, but the degree or strength of interest that is
being measured. The drives or needs revealed in occupational
interests may represent a deeper level of the individual's personality. The occupational interests of the ministry are part and
parcel of the candidate's total striving for a meaningful existence and the actualization of his selfhood.

Studies of Personality

If personality and occupational choices are so closely related,
what about the personalities of individuals who choose the
ministry as an occupation? In general, studies have shown that
emotionally mature and socially aggressive persons tend to be
interested in the type of work represented by the various church
occupations. Ministerial students tend to be sociable in their
interpersonal relations, and meditative in their thinking. They
tend to be relatively free from depression, and to show
adequate emotional stability. They have been shown to be sig-
nificantly above the norms for the average population in ascend-
ancy in social relationships, in friendliness with and thought-
fulness of others, and in a sense of objectivity about themselves.

One study of the assessment of personality of theological
students was conducted to assist a seminary in the screening of
students who had the qualifications for the church-directed
ministry.[32] A functional student personality model most capa-
ble of fulfilling faculty role expectations was developed. The
faculty was asked to provide a list of six students then enrolled
in the seminary, three of whom typified the "ideal" student,
and three considered undesirable. The three ministerial students selected by the theological faculty as "ideal" students
were relatively homogeneous in their control and socially ac-
ceptable channeling of feelings of hostility, in their degree of
personal autonomy, and in their high energy level. They were
basically active persons who were able to persist in achieving
high goals. They were able to respond actively to frustration or

failure, and were not defeated by such disappointments. Their values tended to be directed toward social relationships, and their energy was directed primarily toward persons rather than things. Any introspection or self-examination tended to result in their active influencing of others. Such influence is exercised by persons with internalized sets of goals that have usually been implanted early in life by the significant adults in their lives.

The three students who were judged to be inadequate as ministerial candidates differed radically from the model. Their abilities in social relations were limited, and they lacked sensitivity to others. They tended to lack persistence in achieving their goals, especially when encountering frustration or failure. Value systems tended to be moralistic or legalistic rather than internalized as a set of goals. They also tended to be dependent upon immediate rather than long-term goals.

Something may also be learned about the personality of the ministerial candidates by examining some of their psychological test profiles. The most striking aspects of their test profiles were the emotional patterns expressed in their values, attitudes, and interests. These patterns are labeled as feminine, in a cultural sense, and reflect such attitudes and interests as social values and concern for personal relationships. For the sake of comparison, in the report of the results of the six-year study research in the Institute of Personality Assessment and Research at the University of California, Berkeley, a similar pattern was noted with highly creative persons.[33] The researcher concluded that the more creative a person, the more he tended to reveal an openness to his own feelings and emotions and a wide range of interests, including many that are thought to be feminine in our American culture. In terms of sexual identification and patterns of interests, the more creative subjects appeared to give more expression to the feminine side of their nature than did the less creative persons. There are indications that ministerial candidates show a similar pattern of interests, and in this sense are similar to the creative persons in the study.

The profiles of the ministerial candidates on the occupational interest tests were worth noting. They showed interests similar to those of the psychologist, architect, physician, Y.M.C.A. secretary, social science high school teacher, social worker, and minister. They showed interests most unlike those of the engineer, carpenter, industrial arts teacher, and purchasing agent. These results indicate that the ministerial candidates are relatively uninterested in small details, or in facts for their own sake. They are more concerned with meanings and implications of facts. Their interests in the social-relational fields of work indicate their interest in communicating with others and in relating to them.

Self-perceptions of Ministerial Candidates

Candidates' perceptions of themselves help to indicate additional facets of the relationship between personality factors and the choice of the ministry as an occupation. No comparison studies were made with the self-perceptions of students preparing for other occupations, but some patterns of personality of ministerial candidates are clearly evident. These self-perceptions are descriptions taken from verbatim notes of candidates who were trying to describe themselves:

Candidate 1: "I feel that I have a certain sense of independence. I am concerned about other persons. I have above average abilities though I don't always use them." "I am able to do a job and I am interested in doing something worthwhile in helping others." "I am somewhat independent and I try to be considerate of others."

Candidate 2: "I think that I am honest and serious." "I am seeking, and I study." "I am quiet in crowds, but I am also the life of the party with the gang that I know well." "In regard to my weak points, I don't know what they are. I get along well with people. I try to think through problems. I have determination to go through with my plans." "The only thing I dislike about myself is that I lack in organization of myself, but I don't think it is too bad."

Candidate 3: "I like people. I am easygoing. I haven't had

the push. Possibly I am too easygoing and maybe I should be more prompt. I feel that I am easy to get along with." "I am happy. I am not a grouch. I have a good word generally for others and I feel that I have found myself." "Sometimes I am disappointed that I talk instead of listening. I am trying to be a better listener."

Candidate 4: "I feel that I am a meditative person, that I do serious thinking, but that I am immature and lazy." "I have ability to understand people and I feel that I influence them."

Candidate 5: "I get along well with others and I try to understand other points of view. I worry too much about talking frankly with people. I can say things to people in groups as a speaker can say things, but I have some difficulty in speaking directly to persons." "I feel that I am a jovial guy and get along well with people." "I dislike the fact that I put things off too much."

Candidate 6: "I feel that I am an introvert, but not too much of one. I have an intellectual bent. I like public speaking, I am artistic, and I like to write." "I feel that I have accepted myself, but I am not satisfied with my accomplishments."

Candidate 7: "I feel that I am a stubborn person and dogmatic and have a tendency to argue when I shouldn't." "I am very optimistic. I feel that my weakness is that I am stubborn and dogmatic." "I have an unwillingness to think of my work as work and I have an interest in my work for its own sake." "I value most the acceptance of Christianity which leads to other values. I like my optimism, but it can be a drawback if I am not realistic." "Possibly I am too self-centered."

Candidate 8: "I feel that I am an intense person, high-strung. It's all or nothing with me. I am a perfectionist. No half way." "I have an intense desire to complete things." "I like my persistence, but I dislike the fact that I have a tendency to do things the hard way."

Candidate 9: "I am a fairly friendly person. Sometimes I feel I'm being an intellectual snob. I am moderately good in athletics." "I communicate abstract ideas, but my weakness is that I procrastinate." "In most classes I have a generally good understanding of the subject material." "I like the fact that I am able to do what I like."

Candidate 10: "I feel that I am an average individual. I try to learn and listen to others." "I have a tendency to slack off sometimes. I want to do the job right and to get to the job." "My spiritual experience is what I like, the attitude which is changed, and my new vocational goal." "I am disappointed that I lose my temper."

Candidate 11: "I am pretty even-tempered. I am concerned about others. I am lighthearted and optimistic. I feel that I am a Christian." "I am not very effective with my own family. Maybe people view me as too lighthearted. I am disappointed that I often wait until the last moment and lack discipline." "I like the fact that I can get along well with people in new situations. I like to do my very best."

Candidate 12: "I am a person that doesn't get embarrassed easily. I am easy to get along with. I am not shy but easygoing." "I tend to pass judgment on other people and am not too tolerant, and these are my weaknesses." "My strong points are that I have an ability to get along with others and to make friends. I have a good understanding of others." "I am disappointed in myself that I am kind of jumpy and nervous sometimes."

Candidate 13: "I feel that I get along well with people." "I am disappointed that I am lazy in my studies. I feel that I am pretty intelligent and able to do about anything that I want to do." "I lack discipline, but I like the fact that I can get along with people very well."

Candidate 14: "I am somewhat carefree and easygoing in some respects. I am interested in many things. I stick with an idea and I get along with people. I have self-confidence." "I lack discipline and I often build up little things in my mind which overwhelm me. I lack tact. I desire to do something in school or work and am interested in succeeding in these activities." "Personally, I get along well with others. I like the fact that I am a Christian." "I am disappointed in the discipline of myself in my Christian life."

Candidate 15: "I feel that I am a Christian, first of all." "I feel that I am well-rounded, above average in IQ. I am fairly gentle, but I can rough it up." "I am disappointed that I lack discipline and that I tend to rationalize and that I am not forceful enough." "I feel that I am kind and understanding and I feel with other persons. I am concerned about others. I enjoy meditation and thinking. I am a dreamer." "I dislike the fact that sometimes I do not get on the ball."

Candidate 16: "I have a lot of serious thoughts. I have an ability to convince others, and others confide in me." "I like the fact that I like good books, and that I get along well with other people."

Candidate 17: "I feel that I am a self-centered person, but I desire not to be this way. I feel that I get along well with people and enjoy persons, but sometimes it is difficult to meet persons even though I enjoy it." "I feel that my weakness is that I have an inferiority complex." "I enjoy acting young with kids, and working with persons. I enjoy the fact that I am able to understand, that I have the intellectual capacity. I am physically fit and not ugly." "Sometimes I wish that I were not so loud or that I did not have such a loud mouth."

Candidate 18: "I attempt to be an organized person. I want perfection. I get upset when things don't go the way they should." "I want to be domineering. I am conscientious and I worry too much. I want to get in and work. I never worry about myself, but I am interested in others." "I wish that I wouldn't worry so much."

Candidate 19: "I feel that I am serious. I am concerned about my own life and others. I am introspective. I am concerned and interested in others, and yet I feel that I am also self-centered." "I feel my weakness is that I am self-centered and have a feeling of self-importance. I have the ability to inspire by example in speech and leadership and I am happy that I am never satisfied." "I dislike the fact that I have an interest in myself and a tendency to be a self-centered person."

Candidate 20: "I feel that I am reasonably well-adjusted, and that I have no feeling of inferiority. I have an unsureness of myself in some areas, and I tend to be overpowering in others. I meet persons easily. I like people." "I am glad to be happy rather than sad. I try to communicate with all persons." "I am disappointed in myself when I don't succeed in communicating with others."

These self-perceptions indicate a pattern of interests in working with people. In addition, these men demonstrate an awareness and acceptance of social-relational abilities. They recognize their aptitudes in working with people, their concern for and their desire to help them. They showed a sense of independence and personal autonomy and awareness of personal identity. Predominantly active in temperament, they persist in achieving their goals. They tend to be optimistic in their world view, meditative and introspective in mood, and interested in the realm of ideas. They appear to reflect an essentially serious disposition and a sense of self-confidence.

The Personality of the Ministerial Candidate

Although it is not conclusive, there is considerable evidence to indicate that ministerial students do not differ radically from a typical population of college students in regard to general emotional stability. Such results may be, at least partially, explained by the nature of the ministry within the Protestant tradition. All persons within this tradition are called to a ministry. Where the church calls certain persons to the church-directed ministry, it is a call to specific tasks. It is not so much a call to a profession as it is a call to use personal abilities to fulfill particular needs. The specific needs of the church may change, but the expression of discipleship in vocation remains.

Although the call to a ministry is a call to all Christians, the church calls certain persons with particular "gifts" to use them in the office of the ordained ministry. There is some evidence that these ministerial students tend to be strong in the personal and social traits that are involved in working closely with people in face-to-face relationships. The importance of being able to be autonomous and independent in behavior is noticeable. The minister is involved in decisions that he must make by himself. He needs to be able both to be free from external pressures and to be free *to* act autonomously and vigorously.

The mature ministerial candidate has high goals, and he needs to have the strength of personality to react to the challenge of frustration and failure. A high energy level is expended primarily in the active influencing of persons and situations. He has a secure sense of personal values that he works to communicate through personal and social relationships.

It is clear that an occupational choice cannot be considered apart from personality theory or considerations of motivation. An occupational choice is part of an individual's total striving for a meaningful and purposeful existence. Attitudes, beliefs, needs, and goals are reflected in his choices. The choice of the church-directed ministry is made by a person who tends to be friendly in personal encounter and active in social relationships. He tends to actualize the meaningfulness of a work that involves working closely with the neighbor as an expression of obedience to God.

VII

The Decision-Making Process

DECISION-MAKING is the process by which individuals choose a particular course of action in response to influences upon them. It may involve a personal action, such as choosing which clothes to wear to work, or the choosing of an occupation. The influences may be experienced as coming from outside and not related to the self, or as expressions of a mature understanding of the self.

Every person is responsible for his decisions at particular times and places. The ministerial candidate is responsible for his decisions both in response to his needs and in his choice of goals. The meaningfulness of his existence is involved in self-actualization through the fulfillment of his particular ministry. The fulfillment of his specific ministry depends upon his decision-making in response to the call of vocational obedience and to an occupational choice.

The Background of Decision-Making

Man's conscious self-awareness begins around two years of age, or younger. During the period between one and one-half and four years of age, the child is engaged in what has been characterized by Erik Erickson as the "battle for autonomy." During this time, he not only identifies with his parents' ideas of right and wrong; he also discovers that there are certain

choices that he is free to make. Speaking from the perspective
of developmental psychology, Charlotte Buhler has pointed out
that the "selective responsiveness" of the infant operates from
the beginning of life. The newborn infant is either receptive or
rejective in response to certain foods, sounds, or other stimuli.
Decision-making, or choices, later develop on the basis of comparison. The eight-month-old baby chooses a toy that he can
rattle or swing the best, or the animal that he likes to hug the
best.[34] The realization of one's own potentialities begins in the
choices and decisions of early life. The background for decision-making continues to be formed by the family influences,
socioeconomic and educational background, and the religious
environment of the ministerial candidate. The formative influences upon the candidate help to determine his self-perceptions, which are, in turn, involved in his decision-making.

Decisions regarding basic values expressed in the choice of
identification as a Christian and the concrete choice of the
work of the church's ministry, are both involved in the self-
actualizing needs of the person. Psychologically, each person
makes a particular occupational decision. In attempting to
understand this decision, within the context of the Christian
faith, ministerial candidates may interpret it as a "call." However, the "call to the ministry" is not a matter of fact; it is
theological interpretation of the decision-making process. Psychologically, the decision is involved both in the self-actualizing needs of the person and in the goals that he has set for
himself. In terms of faith, the decision is a response to God in
relation to the concrete reality of the need of the neighbor.
Such a decision involving both dimensions of a student's life
is characterized by openness and affirmation.

Perception in Decision-Making

The process of decision-making involves perceptual factors,
or the way we look at things. These factors may not be ex-
plicitly differentiated by the ministerial candidate making the

decision, but they are usually involved somewhere in the
process. First, there is his perception of the mission and ministry of the church. Regardless of the extent of the limitation or
distortions in his perceptions, some understanding of the
church's ministry is involved in the decision-making. If he
understands that ministry belongs to the whole church, this
will make a difference in his perception of the church-directed
ministry, which will, in turn, influence his decision-making. In
this case, he will need to see himself as involved in ministry
along with others. If he does not understand this ministry as a
shared experience, this perception will influence his decision-
making, in which case he will tend to choose this occupation
in terms of securing a unique privilege or status for himself at
the expense of the ministry of the whole church.

Related to this understanding is the candidate's perception
of the church-directed ministry with its particular occupational
requirements. If he understands that ministry involves a serving of others, this perception will influence his decision-making.
He will then see himself as fulfilling the occupational requirements of a servant who equips others for their ministry. If he
perceives that the primary function of the ordained ministry
is to serve through the teaching and training of others for the
frontline battles of the world, instead of serving in the front
lines himself, his decision-making is affected.

The candidate's perception of himself is also related to the
occupational requirements of the ministry. A person's self-
concept involves the way he perceives himself in relationship
to everything he does. Since the candidate's self-concept involves the way he looks at himself, this perception of his goals
and hopes influences his decision-making. If a candidate has
an exaggerated perception of himself and of his importance, he
will tend to choose the ministry as an occupation in which he
can exert his influence in a highly narcissistic way. A candidate
may have an idealized image of himself that is not at all
realistic. The idealized image is what the subject believes himself to be. It is an unconscious phenomenon, but it represents

the attempt of the person at solving his conflict between what he is and what he wants to be. Karen Horney has indicated that the idealized image is a substitute for realistic self-confidence. This idealized image has a static quality in contrast to authentic ideals. "It is not a goal toward whose attainment he strives, but a fixed idea which he worships."[35] As long as his idealized image remains real to him, "he can feel significant, superior, and harmonious in spite of the illusory nature of those feelings."[36] Such a person is dependent upon the approval and admiration of others to reassure him.

In one study of ministerial candidates, the individual who was judged the most passive and least able of twenty-five subjects made his choice of the ministry as an occupation on the basis of his dreams.[37] In a series of repetitive dreams, he saw himself in an elevated pulpit before the entire congregation. He interpreted this series of dreams as his "call to the ministry." The perception of himself in this way in his dreams means that this individual was not able to perceive himself realistically. He neither knew nor accepted himself as he was, but he made his occupational decision in terms of his perception both of himself and of the role of the minister. Such an individual will not be able to take up a "servant ministry." He will not be able to fulfill the functional demand of a serving ministry. He will not be free to make his witness despite seeming failure, because he will be dependent upon the approval of others. He will depend upon the "professional" criteria of success rather than upon the single criterion of faithfulness.

The Dynamics of the Decision-Making Process

The decision-making process itself involves both the decisions made in reference to specific alternatives and those which are made in the context of a series of other choices and commitments. The decision of a ministerial candidate may depend upon various factors. His choices may be grounded in an understanding of himself and his needs in relationship to the occupational requirements of the ministry, and the needs which the church is called to fulfill in the world. The candidate may evaluate his own abilities and interests in the light of his past experience, and acknowledge that the work of the ministry may be involved in the actualization of his selfhood as he expresses his obedience through his particular ministry.

The decision of the candidate may also be related to the basic commitments that he has already made. A candidate's decision to be obedient to his "calling" comes through the sequence of events within the church and the home, and reflects the work of the Holy Spirit through these channels. Every decision occurs within the context of an ongoing historical process. The ministerial candidate comes to his decision as a person with previous commitments. He has made commitments to the church, to his family and friends, and to any other community to which he belongs. It is in the sequence of these commitments that the occupational decision is made. Consideration of his specific aptitudes and abilities may involve a particular type of decision. Choices made within the sequence of his several commitments will constitute another type of decision. Both types of decision-making are needed to provide the necessary integration of the whole person.

Jesus Christ confronts man at the center, and not at the periphery, of his being. He addresses man as a deciding being, and his decisions become the focus of his true identity. A man's selfhood is centered in his response of commitment in vocation and discipleship. His choice of the ministry as an occupation involves decisions that become the focus of his identity as a person.

In the actual decision-making, there has been considerable misunderstanding about the "call to the ministry." Persons have tended to think that candidates had to attest to some cataclysmic emotional experience as the basis of the "call." In reality, most of the candidates report the gradual nature of their occupational choices, and the series of experiences which surround the decision-making. Indeed, candidates whose decisions were predominantly emotionally oriented tended to drop the ministry as an occupational goal more readily than those whose decisions were made more gradually. On the other hand, the emotional dimension of the candidates' decisions were usually healthy experiences. The influences of emotional factors upon decision-making may be variously interpreted. The emotions experienced in their decisions may tap deep motivational forces within the personality. On the other hand, decisions that are predominantly influenced by emotion tend to be less related to the realistic appraisal of personal abilities, or to the needs of the church and the world. The predominant influence of emotional factors suggest that candidates with these experiences may be governed less by self-actualizing forces, and more by irrational inner pressures or needs.

Each occupation makes particular intellectual and emotional demands upon the person. The churches in the Protestant tradition have certain criteria for the selection of the ministry as an occupation. Under the general classification of the "providential call," they have indicated that ministerial students should have the intellectual and emotional equipment to do the work of the ministry. There is a need of counseling for these candidates to help them to understand the nature of the work of the ministry in relationship to the psychodynamics of their own personalities. The understanding of the relationship between the equipment for the work of the ministry and the nature of the work itself may help some ministerial students to reevaluate their occupational decision.

The decision-making processes may also be examined in counseling with the candidate, in which case, both needs and goals should be explored. It is important to understand if a candidate's decision is prompted by the response to the reality factors of a consideration of his gifts and the needs of the church and of the world. However, his decision may involve his subduing of the reality within himself in a willful plan of self-coercion. He may deny evidence within himself that would make it impossible to meet the occupational requirements of the ministry. Such a self-manipulation would weaken his sensitivity to the leading of the Holy Spirit, which may be expressed through the church's counseling with him about his occupational goal. He may need to be counseled to consider occupational opportunities other than the church-directed ministry.

VIII

The Structure of the Church-directed Ministry

THE STRUCTURE of the church-directed ministry involves the outlines within which this work is performed. Within the Protestant tradition, the ordained ministry is not a matter of mere expediency worked out for the welfare of a human institution. It is a gift from God. It is Christ's gift to the church for the sake of good order. It is a part of the structure of the church, and the function of the pastoral ministry is integral to the body of Christ.

There is a recurring temptation within the church to elevate this ministry to a higher moral order than that of the laity, on one hand, or to fail to recognize the unique functions of the church-directed ministry on the other. The understanding of this ministry as "calling" has led to the kind of misunderstanding reflected in the statement of the mother who said she had hoped her son might have a call from God, but that he had gone into the soap business instead. Candidates for the pastoral ministry often reflect the attitude that a serious commitment to Christian discipleship inevitably involves a call to this particular ministry. However, regardless of the need to discover the ministry of all the people of God, there is also a need to understand the particular structure of the church-directed ministry.

Theological Structure of the Church-directed Ministry

In the New Testament, vocation or "calling" (*klēsis*) refers to God's call to obedience and discipleship. A man is not necessarily called to a particular occupation, but he *is* summoned to work within the church. He is "called" as a teacher or pastor, and as such, is Christ's gift to the church. God's call sets a man apart for a particular work in the church and gives him the necessary "gifts" (*charisma*) to do this work. Paul writes: "And his gifts were that some should be apostles, some prophets, some evangelists, some pastors and teachers" (Eph. 4:11). Having received his summons to this ministry, the candidate responds to what he understands to be God's will for him. As an expression of his obedience, he presents himself to the church for examination, follows its direction in his study and preparation, and seeks ordination to his particular office. The guidance and preparation of the candidate and the service of ordination are acts of the church, and are performed by the ministerial agents of Christ. It is the church that ordains a person to the particular work to which Christ has summoned him.

The nature of this "calling" should provide a check on any professionalism within the ordained ministry. Clergy and laity alike are "called" to do particular tasks within the church. Hence, there is no basis for the conception of the ordained ministry as a higher order of Christian discipleship than that of the laity. However, the ministerial candidate may have also the firm conviction that God has summoned him through the church to serve as a pastoral minister in a work directed by the church. The minister is enabled to take up his work in the confidence that he has been called to his vocation of total discipleship and summoned by the church to his particular task, which is *prior* to the world-directed ministries. He will know that he is ordained to this office by the church through the symbolic affirmation of the "gifts" of ministry, the "laying on of hands." He will understand that he is ordained not to a *higher* order of discipleship, but to a function which is only *prior* to the ministry of all the people of God.

The concept of the *prior* nature of the church-directed ministry is crucial to the recovery of a proper perspective of the pastoral ministry. The function of the ministry within the church and the ministry within the world are of equal importance, but they are not the same in *form*. The *form* of the church-directed ministry is first only in chronology, not in value. The ministry of training and equipping the people of God for their ministry is a *prior* ministry. The work of training the laity for their world-directed ministries is not a *higher* order of ministry, but it is a *prior* ministry.

The report of the deliberations of the Second Assembly of the World Council of Churches in Evanston in 1954 included these words: "The battles of faith today are being fought in the offices, shops and factories, in the political parties, in the press, radio and television." The church-directed ministry may or may not be directly involved in these particular "frontline" battles, but it will most certainly be involved in equipping the laity who are in a position in which they may effectively take up arms in such battles of faith.

The importance of a theologically trained and disciplined ministry cannot be overestimated. If the discipline of theological training and the rigors of self-understanding of the pastoral ministry are not brought to bear upon the training of the laity, their ministry will be fragmented and heretical at best. The church-directed ministry with a disciplined theological training and personal self-understanding will be prepared to fulfill its training functions. Without it, the church's ministry in the world will be irrelevant, because it will understand neither the world nor the gospel.

Without the training by the church-directed ministry, the ministries worked out in the world will be heretical and misleading. The danger of heresy is not so much that something false is being taught, but that *partial* truths are being taught as the *absolute* truth. The *prior* nature of the church-directed

ministry guards against an ill-equipped community of believers carrying a falsely oriented ministry into the world.

There are at least three specific theological dimensions of
such a structure for ministry. Since its nature is derived from
the ministry of Jesus, it is a ministry in mission. The apostles
were the ones who were sent out in mission, and they in turn
sent (*apostellein*) other ministers out. This functional demand
calls for the willingness to prepare others for ministry. It involves a willingness to be sent out, or to train others to be sent
out. It involves a disciplined openness to, and affirmation of,
God's will as it becomes evident in terms of mission. The
church has the responsibility to build itself up not for itself,
but for mission. Indeed, the church is involved in mission as it
prepares the people of God for their ministry.

The ministry in mission is one of service (*diakonia*) to
others. Ministry is service to others, rather than being served
by them. The day of the "prima donna" in the pastoral ministry
is over. It goes without saying that successful "role players"
will continue to attract attention within the Protestant community, but they will be operators of "successful" institutions
rather than servants of the Word. The church-directed ministry
is not so much that of a "headliner," but of a servant or trainer
of others in a shared ministry. This ministry involves a willingness to serve rather than to star. Instead of ordinarily being
involved in the frontline battles himself, he is usually called to
serve in the wings and to prepare others for ministry in the
world.

Another theological function of this ministry is that of
responsible authority (*episcopein*). Within the Protestant tradition, the dimension of the authority of the ministry has been
seriously distorted. The minister is given authority in the sense
that he is assigned particular responsibility. His responsibilities
as prophet, teacher, pastor, or priest involve him in relationships with persons in which the authority of both his person
and his training is brought to bear. Psychologically, he is responsible to the degree that he is able to respond to the neigh-

bor. The theological dimensions of the ministry are not limited to these functions, but they give some guidelines for an outline of the occupational requirements of the pastoral and teaching ministry.

Occupational Structure of the Church-directed Ministry

If the church-directed ministry is to fulfill the purpose provided by its theological structure, ministerial candidates will need to meet certain occupational requirements. Of course, the requirements will vary according to the theological understanding of the nature and mission of the church. Pastoral-seeking committees differ considerably in what they look for in a minister. In reality, what they look for depends upon what they want him for. In the general cultural crisis of this time, the organization of modern society does not provide a clearly relevant place for the minister's distinctive office. With the best of intentions, he is usually thrust into an irrelevant position by the society that surrounds him. The world doesn't know what to do with him, and the church is often confused for the same reason. Unless the church clearly defines the theological structure within which this pastoral, teaching, and priestly ministry is directed, neither the church nor the world will know what to expect from the ministerial office. Unless the church knows what to expect, it certainly won't know what to look for in its ministers.

If the work of the church-directed ministry is one of training others, then it is necessary to provide them with a certain kind of professional training. While this *form* of ministry is never devoid of the personal dimension, it is necessary to equip this ministry in the use of professional tools for the proper work of this particular occupation. A particular kind of student is needed to fulfill the requirements of this structured ministry. A student with certain psychological and intellectual equipment is needed to work within the structure provided for the church-directed ministry.

The pastoral ministry today takes many forms that were not considered in an earlier agrarian culture. It was relatively simple to describe the form and function of a pastor in a rural community. However, a culture that is in the midst of rapid changes requires numerous forms of special ministries. There are the ministries that change according to the needs of the suburb, the inner city, the university community, or the hospital community. Each of these special situations requires a specialized form of ministry. However, despite the particular form in which it may be expressed, all these special ministries have a generalist nature. The integrative function of these pastoral ministries require a generalist frame of reference rather than that of the specialist. Although the forms of service and the strategies may vary according to the needs of the particular situation, the function of the pastoral ministry is of a general nature. He works to bind together those things which are scattered and at loose ends. As in the Latin root of the word "religion" (*relegere*), the pastoral ministry works "to gather again," or "to gather back (again)." Hence, the ministerial student must be able to fulfill the function of a generalist in our culture. Although various types of abilities are needed to fulfill the specialized needs, the structure of the pastoral ministry as an occupation is integrative and generalist in nature.

In general, some occupational requirements are evident in the personal relationships between the minister and his parishioners. Although such needs may be expressed at an unconscious level, the community of believers need a secure person around whom they can experience some sense of belonging or "life together." Since all the people of God have a ministry, they all have the responsibility to minister to each other. Nevertheless, the healthiness of the relatedness between the members of the community of faith is partly dependent upon the secure sense of relatedness between pastor and parishioner. An integral part of the pastor's work involves his selfhood, which has both personal and spiritual dimensions. The point at which his private life begins and his professional duties end is constantly changing, and anxiety may be aroused both

within himself and within the parishioners as he seeks to discover his unique function. The ministerial candidate needs to
be a person with sufficient self-understanding to be able to
work at a level of depth in personal involvement with people
and still retain a sense of personal psychological integrity.

There are a number of specific personal requirements to look
for in the ministerial candidate. He needs to have an understanding of himself in terms of his sexual identity. Since he
will be involved in interpersonal relationships with both men
and women in his pastoral, teaching, and administrative roles,
he needs to be sufficiently free from emotional distortions to
be able to relate without projecting his own insecurities and
inadequacies upon the other person. To the extent that he is
unaware of the meaning of his masculine identity, he will tend
to exploit persons for his own unmet needs, rather than to
relate with and minister to them.

The ministerial candidate needs to understand himself in
terms of his aggressiveness. If he has developed an attitude of
aggression toward others in order to get results, he will tend
to exploit others rather than to be caught at a disadvantage.
He will tend to destroy others through his relationships with
them rather than to modify his own behavior patterns. He may
overwhelm his parishioners through some action-oriented program, but he will tend to use them and to be more concerned
with the results than with the means to achieve them.

The dimensions of authority of the church-directed ministry
also need to be understood. There is an authority to every person's ministry. Although one's ministry is not to be equated
with Christ's, it is not altogether separate from it. The authority of the ministry of all the people of God comes from Christ,
and it is not so much expressed through an institutional authority as through the meaningful relationships of "life together."
The authority of the minister of Christ comes only from the
one who lives under authority to Christ. Jesus Christ is "being
formed in us" as we are obedient to him and as we relate to
one another.

The ordained minister has this authority given to him by

God, and he also has particular authority granted by the community of believers. In the Protestant tradition, authority is delegated responsibility. The function of training and "equipping the saints" involves the authority of his theological training and commitment. He has been equipped by the "doctors" of the church to train the community of believers for their work of ministry in the world. His theological education prepares him to communicate the wholeness of the teachings of the church, and to guard against the heresies of partial and fragmented truths. The authority of his ordination commitment places him under the authority of the church through the structures of the congregation, presbytery, or bishop. The ministerial candidate needs to encounter the authority of Christ, and to be able to accept his own authority as the result of that encounter. The acceptance of this authority involves accepting both the authority granted by the church, and the personal authority of his commitments and of the strengths and limitations of his selfhood. The candidate who has not accepted the authority that is uniquely his will tend to become a "salesman" of "eternal goods" rather than the representative of Jesus Christ.

While the ordained minister has particular authority delegated to him, the insecure persons of our time seek an authoritarian symbol that will grant them a haven secure from life's troublesome questions. Many church members expect their minister "to have all the answers." They evade their responsibility to prepare themselves for their ministry by employing a professional "answer man" who is paid to give them answers without too much effort on their part. However, the authority of the minister is not to give "pat answers" to questions of human predicament. These are the questions with which everyone has to wrestle for himself. The authority of the ordained minister is not that of the witch doctor but of the teacher. His authority lies in his understanding of the world and of himself. His theological training and his personal understanding equip him to help others to wrestle with their questions of human predicament. He is equipped to help them to examine their questions rather than to evade or deny them. However, he is not equipped in the sense in which he no longer needs to wrestle with the same problems himself. Meeting crises in his teaching and in his pastoral care may involve the minister himself in a personal crisis of faith. Such a crisis may also be the means by which others may be encouraged to meet a similar crisis in their own faith.

In a more general sense, the ministerial candidate needs to respond to the "call to be a Christian," which is the first dimension of his call to the ministry. In response to this call, he needs to have some experience of the acceptance of Christ. Without a personal experience of the good news that God loves him and accepts him as he is without merit, he will be unable to speak of the acceptance to which the church witnesses as it proclaims the gospel.

Furthermore, a personal knowledge of guilt and forgiveness is important to the person who is asked to represent Jesus Christ and the community of believers in the communication of forgiveness. The ministerial candidate needs to know both the meaning of forgiveness and the difference between real and neurotic guilt in his own existence. Such a personal knowledge will enable him to communicate the grace and forgiveness of Jesus Christ to the persons to whom he ministers.

Psychological Structure of the Church-directed Ministry

The relationship between personality and the choice of the ministry as an occupation may be studied from various perspectives. The church has always recognized that there are different motivations for choosing the ministry, and that there are particular occupational requirements of the church-directed ministry. A complete study of the problems of a program of counseling ministerial candidates cannot be included here. Nor is there any intention of including an exhaustive examination of the requirements of the work of the pastoral ministry. The following dimensions of the ministry as an occupation are included to indicate the general direction for the recruiting of, and the counseling with, ministerial candidates.

One study of personality factors in the choice of the Protestant ministry as an occupation showed that in comparison with college students in various classes, seminary students were more guilt ridden, had more difficulty with sexual and hostile feelings, and were more intrapunitive. These results point up some crucial problems of the relationship between personality and the occupation of the ministry, but the meaning of these results needs to be carefully evaluated. The researcher was careful to point out that the origin of an occupational choice cannot invalidate the meaning of the choice itself. The identification of unconscious motivations is helpful in the counseling of ministerial candidates for the purpose of increased self-understanding. However, the concept of functional autonomy of motivation, as developed by Gordon Allport, indicates that a change in goals takes place as growth occurs. The motivating factors that have had the goal of alleviating a sense of guilt by service to the church through the ministry may become functionally autonomous in the sense that they become independent of their origin. However, although motives may be independent of their origin, they are not independent of the ego structure of the individual. Hence, a primary concern involves the consideration of the structure of personality. The fundamental problem in the psychological analysis and evaluation of the ministerial candidate is not dependent upon the genesis of a choice, but upon the personality structure of the individual.

In general, the occupational requirements of the ordained ministry involve a structure of personality that may be characterized as active rather than passive. By way of definition, the active person is one who seeks a deeper understanding of the essential elements of his own personality, interests, capacities, and values to which he desires to give expression. A passive person acts as if decisions are to be made for him by someone else, or that they should be the more or less inevitable outcome of his current experiences. He feels that there is relatively little he can do to determine the outcome of any enterprise in which he is involved. When an opportunity is offered, he may grasp it, but he will do little to create one on his own. The active person is not as dependent upon ego needs as the passive person, and he tends to show persistence in goal achievement. He is able to forgo current gratifications or to postpone them, and he attempts to find expression for his inner drives and to actualize himself through his work.

In terms of specific behavioral expressions of the active structure of personality, the active person has, first of all, a healthy sense of autonomy and independence. He is not a person who needs to feed upon others but is able to bear the burdens of others. A passive person tends to be dependent upon an idealized self which substitutes for a realistic self-confidence. The idealized self is not a goal toward which he strives, but it is a fixed idea which he worships. As long as this image remains real to him he can feel significant or superior, in spite of the illusory nature of those feelings. Such a person is dependent upon the approval and admiration of others to reassure him.

Secondly, the active person has a high energy level. He is not necessarily an activist, because intelligence is also a form of energy. However, his energy is directed toward socially constructive goals in relation to the active influencing of persons in terms of the values that he represents. He is able to respond to various types of demands upon his energy and to be involved in a variety of projects concurrently. His energy is expressed not only through involvement with the demands of others upon him, but also in the discipline of his mind through independent study and meditation. The high level of energy provides the basis for occupational integration at a depth not available to the person with a more limited energy level.

The active person also has a high frustration tolerance. He is able to react with resilience when confronted with frustration and/or failure. He is not dependent upon immediately achieving goals, but is able to formulate long-range goals and to work toward them. Encountering difficulties in working toward his goals, the active person interprets them as challenges rather than simply as frustrations. He tends to be counteractive in response to frustrations rather than withdrawing from them.

In addition, the active person has a sufficient degree of self-understanding to be free to do his best work. He understands himself in terms of his sexual identity. He is sufficiently free from his own needs so that he does not primarily seek comfort from others in his pastoral relationships. He is relatively free from the projection of his own insecurities onto the other person. This active person has sufficient self-understanding to be able to be open to his own feelings and emotions, and he is free to give expression to a wide range of interests. He is able to give range to the feminine side of his nature rather than denying expression to the culturally derived feminine values. He understands himself in terms of his aggressiveness so he will not need to exploit others to achieve results.

The active person also has some particular characteristics, which are directly counter to those of the passive individual, that may be described as penetrating reality and thus encountering a world of possibilities which would never occur to the passive person. These differences with which the ministerial candidate approaches his problems and decisions are usually developed early in life and are fairly stable factors in personality structure and motivational patterns. Charlotte Buhler observed that active babies showed curiosity and a certain courage in tackling new stimuli, while babies who were afraid and withdrew from new stimuli showed a more passive behavior. She concluded that the active baby anticipates a positive reality, while a passive infant anticipates a negative reality, and that these patterns of behavior tend to persist throughout adult life.

The self-perceptions of ministerial candidates provide an

additional dimension for understanding the occupational requirements of the ministry. How a person thinks of himself determines largely what he does. His choice of occupation is influenced greatly by his self-concept. The self-concept is a major determinant in occupational choice, and such a choice provides the way an individual can express his concept of self in work. A self-concept is the way a person looks at himself. It includes his feelings, goals, ideals, hopes, ambition, and the way he looks at himself in relation to anything he does. The role is what a person does, and the occupational role is the implementation of the way a person looks at himself.

The self-perceptions of ministerial candidates provide helpful descriptions of what we are looking for in a minister. Verbatim notes of interviews with candidates who did *not* persist in goal achievement have some interesting similarities. In their comments, they tend to lack persistence in goal achievement and to perceive themselves as tending to procrastinate and to be lacking in personal discipline. These candidates may be persons who get along well with others, but they seem to lack the ability to pursue their goals in a disciplined fashion. They may tend to be optimistic by nature, but they also tend to be unrealistic about what can be accomplished.

A random selection of the self-perceptions of the ministerial candidates who *did* persist in goal achievement shows some demonstrable differences compared with those who did not. These candidates express persistence in goal achievement. They demonstrate a healthy acceptance of themselves. They tend to accept both their strengths and their weaknesses. Their responses show a healthy acceptance of positive feelings about themselves. In addition, these candidates appear to be more actively oriented and more involved in long-term rather than immediate goals. Such candidates appear to be more oriented toward the work of the ministry rather than being dependent upon the meeting of ego needs through achieving immediate goals. Since the minister rarely sees the immediate results of his work, he needs to be the kind of person who can tolerate work goals that are long-range and those which cannot be immediately achieved. He needs to be the kind of person who can encounter frustration and temporary failure, and to be able to rebound rather than to capitulate to defeat.

In general, the self-perceptions of the able ministerial candidates indicate a pattern of interests of working with people. They demonstrate an awareness and acceptance of social-relational abilities. They recognize their aptitudes in working with people, and their concern for and their desire to help them. They show a sense of independence and personal autonomy and an awareness of personal identity. Predominantly active in temperament, they tend to persist in goal achievement. They tend to be optimistic in their world view, meditative and introspective in mood, and interested in the realm of ideas. They reflect an essentially serious disposition, and some sense of self-confidence.

Intellectual Structure of the Church-directed Ministry

The ministerial candidate also needs to prepare himself to meet the intellectual requirements of this ministry. In his preparation, he will need to be able to think clearly and to develop some skill in verbal expression. Ideas and words are his tools. Although the intellectual demands may vary with the denomination, in the Protestant tradition there is a continual emphasis upon academic excellence. Three years of graduate work in a theological school is the standard requirement to prepare for the work of the church-directed ministry. The basic requirement for pre-seminary preparation is an education in the liberal arts. Although the major area of study may vary, college courses should include certain factors. The American Association of Theological Schools has prepared a statement on "The Function of Pre-Seminary Studies," which points out the kind of results which a ministerial candidate should be able to show from his college studies:

College courses prior to theological seminary should provide the cultural and intellectual foundations essential to an effective theological education. They should issue in at least three broad kinds of attainment.

1. The college work of a pre-seminary student should result in the ability to use certain tools of the educated man:

    (a) The ability to write and speak English clearly and correctly. English composition should have this as a specific purpose, but this purpose should also be cultivated in all written work.

    (b) The ability to think clearly. In some persons this ability is cultivated through courses in philosophy or specifically in logic. In others, it is cultivated by the use of the scientific method, or by dealing with critical problems in connection with literary and historical documents.

    (c) The ability to read at least one foreign language and in some circumstances more than one.

2. The college work of a pre-seminary student should result in increased understanding of the world in which he lives:

    (a) The world of men and ideas. This includes knowledge of English literature, philosophy, and psychology.

    (b) The world of nature. This is provided by knowledge of the natural sciences, including laboratory work.

    (c) The world of human affairs. This is aided by knowledge of history and the social sciences.

3. The college work of a pre-seminary student should result in a sense of achievement:

    (a) The degree of his mastery of his field of study is more important than the credits and grades which he accumulates.

    (b) The sense of achievement may be encouraged through academic concentration, or through "honors" work, or through other plans for increasingly independent work with as much initiative on the student's part as he is able to use with profit.

Although the comparative value of academic majors varies somewhat according to the particular college or university, the ministerial candidate should be able to do his major work in either philosophy, English, history, psychology, or sociology.

Regardless of the major field of specialization in college, no candidate for the ministry should enter seminary without a thorough grounding in various courses within these major areas of study. In philosophy, he should include such courses as contemporary and history of philosophy. A knowledge of the answers men have given and are giving to life's deepest questions is indispensable if the candidate is to understand those to whom he is called to preach the gospel. The area of philosophy helps to provide this kind of knowledge.

While extensive studies in the field of religion in college are not necessary, it is important that a candidate for the ministry have a basic understanding of the field of study into which he will enter in seminary. This includes a knowledge of the Bible, and the historical approach to its understanding. He needs a sound knowledge of philosophy of religion, particularly an acquaintance with the main theological positions in contemporary Christian thought. He will need an adequate appreciation of ethics, including an understanding of the attempts to apply the implications of the gospel in personal life and social experience.

Since the gospel must be apprehended and appropriated by individuals, candidates for the ministry should know what the science of psychology can contribute to the understanding of persons and interpersonal relations. Help toward such an understanding may be secured from courses in child or developmental psychology, and abnormal psychology or mental hygiene.

Since individuals live their lives in patterns of social relationships in social institutions, courses in social psychology or social institutions are important to help the ministerial candidate to understand both social relationships and the institutions in which they take place.

Since our knowledge of the life of man in all of its richness, complexity, and depth is acquired chiefly through literature and history, preparation for the ministry should include all the courses in the area of English and history that the candidate can possibly take in the light of other needs. Most colleges have particular requirements in these areas for all students.

Colleges differ in their offerings, and the candidate will need to take these recommendations into consideration when deciding upon an institution for undergraduate study. If, of necessity, he takes his work in an institution where such courses are not available, he should plan to acquire them through summer courses or directed personal study. In all of this work, he needs to strive for a B average as a minimum goal for his undergraduate work.

In general, the more able candidate can meet the psychological and intellectual requirements of the ministry. Since he is more work-oriented, he will tend to find satisfaction in fulfilling both the psychological and intellectual demands that are made upon him in the performance of his work. The less able candidate will tend to look for the kind of psychological satisfaction that will give him ego support. Compensating for intellectual or personal inadequacies, he will tend to be domineering as a means of expressing the necessary qualities of leadership demanded by the work of the church-directed ministry.

The Structure for the Fulfillment of the Church-directed Ministry

The structure for the fulfillment of the church-directed ministry involves the theological bases of the "call to the ministry" and the personal, psychological, and intellectual dimensions of this form of ministry. The "call" comes from God; but it comes through the church. It is the responsibility of the entire community of believers to participate both in the calling and in the ordering of the church-directed ministry in terms of where the ministry is to be performed, the service that it is to render, and the delegated responsibility to do the work.

The church is responsible for examining the ministerial candidate in terms of his personal, psychological, and intellectual fitness to fulfill the kind of ministry that is ordered by the church. Whether or not he is able to fulfill the occupational requirements of this ministry is dependent upon the providence of God. In the Protestant tradition, the church has always insisted that if a man has been called to the church-directed ministry, it is within the providence of God to endow him with the requisite abilities or "gifts" (*charisma*) to fulfill this ministry. Hence, the church is fulfilling its responsibility as it examines ministerial candidates to determine whether or not they are able to meet the necessary occupational requirements.

It may be helpful to recall at this point that the "call to the ministry" is not a matter of fact, but is an interpretation of a series of complex human experiences. Therefore, from the scientific standpoint, psychological facts should be used in helping the community of believers to understand the complexity of the ministerial candidate and his motivation. However, it must be reaffirmed that it is not within the province of the psychologist to make the final judgment in regard to a "call." He cannot validate a "call to the ministry" in a theological sense; but he can help the church to evaluate the "call" by contributing to the understanding of the person and his motivation, both of which are dimensions of the structure of the ministry as an occupation.

IX

The Church's Guidance of the Ministerial Candidate

THE CHURCH'S GUIDANCE of ministerial candidates begins with both an understanding of the nature of vocation and an interpretation of the "call to the ministry" as an occupational option that comes within the context of Christian vocation. The actual program of guidance involves the confronting of persons with the possible occupational choices, and the counseling that follows any decision-making.

Since the "call to the ministry" comes through the church, it has a primary responsibility to call out its able young men and women to fulfill particular functions within the community of believers. While the church has always needed more able leaders than it has had, the present decade will mark a critical period in its history. The people of God are confronted with the problem of challenging their most able youth and adults to respond to the need for theological leadership. It is not a problem of numbers, but of quality of commitment of heart and mind. While many reasons have been given for the failure of the church to meet this challenge to provide theological leadership for the church, a recent report of the Congregational churches of England points up the primary problem. "This commission believes that recruitment for the ministry will be best helped as Church members . . . recover a clear understanding of the purpose and functions of the Church and its ministry as servants of the Gospel in the contemporary world."[38] It is the responsibility of the entire community of believers to fulfill their ministry within the world and to provide for the ministry within the church. It is the church that calls out persons to serve in a particular function, but it is God who endows them with the "gifts" (*charisma*) of ministry which can be expressed in the service of the church.

The active participation of the whole church in calling persons to give serious consideration to the ministry as an occupation does not involve the emotional exploitation of youth in summer conferences. It is simply the recognition of the responsibility of the community of believers to work toward the provision of a pastoral ministry equal to the task of the twentieth century. The responsibility of the church is clearly defined in reference to the examination of the "gifts" of ministry within the "providential" dimension of the "call to the ministry." The church needs its most able youth and adults for theological leadership within the local parishes. Every time a weak ministerial candidate is accepted, the church is saying both to the world and to its most able young adults that it is content with mediocrity. The higher the requirements for the pastoral ministry, the more seriously will the call be heeded by able young men and women.

Both the report of the Congregational churches of England referred to earlier and similar reports in the U.S.A. emphasize the crucial importance of the participation of the local church in recruitment for the church-directed ministry. It has been interesting to observe that some churches tend to have many more ministerial candidates than others. Some pastors and congregations are actively involved in the guidance and counseling of young men and women who are considering the pastoral ministry as an occupation, and others are doing little or nothing about it. Regardless of the extent of the denominational program in the guidance of ministerial candidates, the involvement of the local church is crucial.

Program of Guidance in the Local Church

In reaction against emotional pressure and exploitation of youth and young adults, the church has tended to be apologetic about confronting particular persons within the community of believers with the challenge of the pastoral ministry. God's call, as well as his concern, is usually expressed through persons. The community of believers has a responsibility and an opportunity to confront both youth and adults to consider this ministry as a live occupational option. Although it does not prove anything conclusively, it is interesting how many ministerial candidates recall that someone had once asked them, "Have you ever considered the ordained ministry?" It is difficult to evaluate the extent of the influence of such a question, but the fact that so many ministerial candidates have mentioned such incidents is indicative of a recall which seems to be more than coincidental.

Regardless of the extent of the influence of an isolated suggestion to consider the pastoral ministry as an occupational option, there are some unique opportunities available to the church in the area of occupational guidance. One of the important areas in such guidance which is often neglected is that of group work. Ordinarily, group occupational guidance is concerned with providing occupational information, the broadening of occupational understanding, and the stimulation of interest in occupational planning. The church has an unusual opportunity in this area. One of the primary concerns of the church is that of Christian education. Groups of young people of various ages participate in both the structured classes of the church school and in the more informal discussions of the youth fellowship meetings. The church has the opportunity of relating the faith of the individual to the idea of Christian vocation through its church school curricula. In the informal discussion groups, young people may be introduced to persons in various ministries, directed either by the church or by the world. A study series on the meaning of Christian vocation may be planned with special reference to the various types of occupations, whether church-directed or world-directed.

Another type of group approach that is being used successfully is the series of meetings in which the emphasis is placed upon a permissive group interaction. The importance of the exploration of feelings about occupational goals is stressed. This group experience allows young people the freedom to explore the nature of their goals through informal discussions. The meetings are structured informally. "Going around" with a simple question about their understanding of their "call" provides the means by which each student may participate on the same level. In the discussion which follows, the students begin to talk about some of the questions that they have encountered in their quest to discover God's will in vocation and, in particular, their choice of the ministry as an occupation. They talk about some of their doubts regarding their own decisions. The purpose of the discussions is the clarification and understanding of one's self in terms of one's occupational goal. The group experience helps each of them to be realistic about themselves and their goals. Since some occupational decisions disregard many of the realities of the situation facing a person, the group may help an individual to test his decision through further experience.

Regional summer and winter conferences provide additional opportunities for group occupational guidance. Pastors in the local church and on the university campus are in a position where they help to direct these conferences. They can plan programs that will interpret Christian vocation in general and church occupations in particular. Several different types of approach have been made in such conferences. One effective way has included the combination of a continuing study group and occupational testing by someone who is trained to interpret such tests. The study group makes it possible for young people to consider the Biblical and theological basis of Christian vocation. Study about the nature of the work of the church in the contemporary world enables them to understand the occupational requirements of the church-directed ministry in the day in which they live. The testing may be an integral part of the study group. These psychometric devices may increase the student's interest in occupational possibilities and help them to clarify their understanding of themselves in relation to the requirements of a particular occupation. In some conferences in which this approach was used, each student took the tests, the nature and purpose of the tests were discussed in the group as a whole, and individual counseling was made available for anyone who wished it. Occupational counselors have been invited to participate in such study groups either as regular faculty members or as special consultants to work with a theologically trained minister who might conduct the study group. Ministers and university pastors who have had at least a minimum of training in psychology and psychometric testing may be able both to advise study groups and to administer tests and do the necessary counseling. Available facilities in the community and on the campus may be suggested to those desiring further testing and counseling, especially in reference to the guidance counselor in the public schools or in the community colleges.

Another pattern for group study could be the showing of films or filmstrips that relate to the understanding of Christian vocation, and with special reference to church occupations. Questions resulting from the showing of the film may lead to some worthwhile exploration of the problem of occupational decision.

Group work is one of the important elements of any church program. It is a methodology that is available to churches regardless of the location or size of membership. Furthermore, persons are often more accessible through groups than through individual counseling. Since the group experience provides for the expression of the "priesthood of all believers," members of the congregation are enabled to "minister" to each other through their occupational study. They may help their neighbor and be helped by their neighbors in relating faith to work and in understanding themselves in relationship to others.

In addition to the usual programs of Christian education in

the church school and the youth fellowship, some churches
have initiated special programs of occupational guidance
aimed toward all the youth and young adults in the congregation. Any program of guidance of ministerial candidates should
be conducted within the context of a total vocational concern
for the youth or young adults of the church. Some churches
have initiated interviews with every young person as he
reaches the junior year in high school. He is interviewed about
his educational and occupational plans. In this way every
young person is given an opportunity for such an interview
before he graduates from high school. Setting up an occupational guidance section in the church library, a career night for
youth, or a parent-teacher meeting on occupational choices
may be helpful ways to interpret the program of guidance to
the entire congregation. All such programs would certainly be
of help to young people who are involved both in the process
of discovering the meaning of Christian vocation and in the
determination of the direction of their occupational choices.

The Focus of the Guidance Process

Occupational guidance includes the principles of any good
counseling. Trust in the counselor is one of the first requisites
of rapport. This trust is not earned through cleverness or
through subtle cajolery; it is a gift that is given in response to
respect. If the attitude of the counselor is one of genuine
respect for the person, the techniques that he uses are of
secondary importance.

The wholesome counseling relationship is characterized by
the attitude of respect and acceptance of the person as he is
without any preconceived notion of what he should be. The
meaning of respect may be traced to the root of the word,
respicere, to look at. It means the ability to see the person as
he is. It means being aware of the unique individuality of a
person, and the willingness to let him grow as he is. There is
the attitude of the counselor that allows the person freedom to

discover new insights according to his own tastes. The individual's autonomy is accepted and the counselor helps him to accept responsibility for himself.

The counselor of persons who seek occupational help will be tempted to depend upon giving advice and reassurance. Someone has remarked that it is not safe to give advice unless you can be sure that the other person will not heed it. Ordinarily, the individual does not primarily need advice. He may need additional information in order to make his decision. Referral for tests and counseling may prove helpful in some instances, especially referrals to the public school guidance counselor. However, his chief need is to establish a harmony between his occupational aspirations and the reality of his capacities. He needs to be free *from* the anxiety that blocks his undertakings, and free *to* mobilize his capacities for purposeful ends.

When the counselor gives in to the temptation to offer advice, in reality he may deny the individual the opportunity to come to grips with himself. He takes over for the person and arrives at a solution (advice) that is not necessarily related to the particular individual involved. Occupational guidance is not predicated upon certain static principles that can be applied with a regularity of laws. On the contrary, it is based upon the approach that there is an individual answer for each person.

The focus of all guidance is that it is a helping discipline. The function of the counselor in the church's program is to assist the individual in the discovery of the occupational area in which he will be able to meet the greatest need in the world which God has given him, and to work with the greatest sense of personal fulfillment in meeting the need and in the use of his abilities. Such guidance involves more than learning techniques and principles that can be applied with routine regularity to individuals falling in certain categories. Guidance involves the active use of self. It is a pastoral function that means personal involvement of one's self in working toward the actualization of the selfhood of another. It involves more than technical knowledge of testing and job analysis; it is concerned with the consideration of the individual's needs and goals. It involves the individual's emotional acceptance of himself and his occupational goals.

The concern of the counselor is that persons may mobilize their own inner resources to the optimum. In the process of reaching this goal, it is usually necessary for the individual to verbalize his feelings. Hence, the function of the counselor is to help the person to talk freely in a relationship of acceptance and understanding. He will need to increase his understanding of his own abilities and to develop his appreciation of the need of the particular work directed by the church.

Anyone exploring occupational possibilities may experience a certain degree of ambivalence. On the one hand, there is the problem of choice that disturbs him. On the other hand, he is afraid to involve himself in the process of working toward the decision. The fear of personal involvement may lead persons to insist that psychometric tests be administered to them. Some persons may hope that the answer to their problem lies in the impersonal and objective tests. They don't want to be involved in a personal struggle with their occupational decision. They want their problem solved without any involvement of self with self, of self with others, or of self with God.

There is always some anxiety in any genuine counseling, but the function of the counselor is to help the person to recognize his conflicting feelings and to accept them as part of his real self. Hence, the process of occupational assistance is one of growth that involves the discovery, the increased understanding, and the affirmation of the individual's own strength in terms of his chosen goals.

A young person usually has quite a variety of occupational interests that challenge him. He is curious about what he wants to do in life, but he rarely has a clear understanding of himself in relation to his occupational aspirations. A teen-ager is preoccupied with the problem of defining himself as independent

4.5086

from his parents, while the young adult may have narrowed the field of occupational possibilities somewhat. At this point of young adulthood, the individual is probably free from some of the emotional conflicts of adolescence and is now free to put his mind to constructive and purposeful attainment.

A teen-ager is often a study in contradiction. Since he has had only a limited amount of experience, he is optimistic about the nature of his future. There is an openness to occupational guidance, because the world offers unlimited opportunities for achievement. He is eager to discover what life has in store for him. At the same time, because of the limited nature of his experience, he is unsure of himself in an adult world. His anxieties also bring an openness to guidance, and he may be very open to the search for God's will in occupation. The tension developing from his anxieties drives him to seek clarification and understanding.

Since a young person has a limited experience of the world about him, he may be moved to make an occupational decision through an emotional experience. Such a decision may disregard much of the reality that must be tested through further experience. It is the opportunity of the counselor to help the young person to test himself against the realities of the world surrounding him. While the emotional decision may tap deep motivational forces within him, the clarification achieved through counseling is a necessary adjustment both to the realities of the world's need and of his personal capacities.

Some young people have already made occupational decisions prior to any guidance provided by the church. These young people may have been influenced in a variety of immature ways. Their fathers may have wanted them to go into some church-directed work, or a mother may have wanted one of her sons to be a minister. Other parents will have higher aspirations for their children than they had been able to achieve. On the other hand, the individual may have thought out his occupational goals very carefully. He may have taken some psychometric tests in high school that indicated a par-

Lincoln Christian College

ticular pattern of occupational interests. Such a person may believe that he has made the only logical decision. However, any counselor knows that the interests and goals of young people may change considerably as experience is gained. Hence, occupational goals need continual reexamination. Indeed, the job of guidance is not completed simply with the inclusion of a few psychometric tests, as important as these may be, in helping the individual to evaluate himself in terms of a particular occupational goal.

By being sensitive to some of the nuances of the individual's behavior in both individual and group situations, the counselor may help him to reexamine his occupational goal. There are several different types of behavior to which the counselor and/or official boards may be sensitive. First, there is the question of his social behavior. How well does he get along in social relationships? Does he have many friends? Does he seem to prefer solitary work to any group activities? Does he enjoy working with others? Does he ever take any positions of leadership, or is he always submissive to another's leadership? The answers to such questions may enable the counselor to understand the individual in relation to his aspirations. It may be quite apparent that he is unfitted for a position which involves working closely with people, and yet because of his unconscious motivations, he is determined to go ahead with his occupational plans. His mother's desire to have a son in the ministry may be the source of motivation that keeps him from understanding himself. He may even influence the outcome of the psychometric tests unconsciously through this false picture of himself.

A second type of behavior to observe is that of temperament or the pattern of emotional reaction. How well does he respond to the routine aspects of an activity? Is he methodical in his approach to problems, or is he impulsive in his approach? Is he more concerned with the broad nature of a problem, or with the details? The answers to some of these questions indicate something about the nature of the occupation in which a particular person will find a sense of purpose and self-fulfillment.

An individual whose primary concern is with details will usually be emotionally unsuited for a task involving the broad outlines. A methodical person needs an occupation in which his temperament will find the most complete expression. Ordinarily, a potential ministerial candidate will tend to be more concerned with the broad nature of a problem than with the details. While he may be able to handle routine aspects of an activity, he needs to be responsive to new forms of activities. He needs to be able to initiate new forms of ministry in the world rather than to simply improve on the routine of managing an established institution.

The way a person's mind works is a further type of behavior to observe. Is he able to express himself well? Is he interested in verbal expression? Can he use words as tools? Is he inclined to be reflective about some of the broad social problems? The type of mental behavior that characterizes a particular individual will say a great deal about the type of occupation which is suited to his mental makeup. Since individuality and the freedom with which God calls cannot be categorized, it is possible for a person to contradict many of the generalizations of guidance, but the way a person's mind works is at least one of the indications of his occupational fitness for the pastoral ministry. The potential ministerial candidate tends to have both interest and ability in verbal expression, and the more able candidate appears to be reflective about personal and social issues. While it is true that God is not limited by any generalized rules of occupational guidance, it appears that God usually works through the different types of human behavior. God seems to work through the uniqueness of each mind and personality. Ordinarily, he does not seem to circumvent the social, mental, and emotional makeup of the individual in any call to discipleship.

Conducting the Interview

Some concrete suggestions may be helpful for the counselor in any program of guidance. Of course, the context of counsel-

ing with youth and young adults will vary according to the
purpose of the particular interview. In one situation, the pastor
or the church officer may initiate the guidance process by
scheduling interviews with every young person in a particular
class, such as an interview with a young person by the time
he reaches the junior class in high school. In another instance,
the pastor may learn of an interest in the ministry that had
been expressed during a church school class, work project, or
summer conference. In the latter instance, it is important for
the pastor to talk to the young person himself first and to tell
him about the source of his information. Regardless of the
original reason for the interview, if he expresses some interest
in the ministry as an occupation, he should be encouraged to
talk about his interests and what has led up to them. He will
need to talk about his understanding of the pastoral ministry,
and what aptitudes he thinks he can bring to such work. It may
be helpful for him to talk about those who have influenced
him, and how his interests have been stimulated. He will need
to examine his parents' response to his interests, and how their
response is related to these interests. Ministerial candidates
have at times reflected uncritically the parents' interest in the
pastoral ministry. On the other hand, some ministerial candidates have sought, albeit unconsciously, an occupation that
would be totally rejected by their parents.

In addition to the exploration of occupational interests, the
counselor may suggest certain resources to provide the necessary information about occupational requirements. Some books
and periodicals may be suggested to broaden the person's
understanding about the nature of the pastoral ministry as an
occupation. Since one of the chief occupational requirements
of this ministry is self-understanding, any possible avenues for
such interpersonal exploration should be provided. Individual
and group counseling on a formal or informal basis, the usual
pastoral care and friendship, an informal sharing in bull
sessions, or any other way of exploring the means of selfhood
should be initiated by the community of believers for their
ministerial candidates.

The church counselor should also suggest that the guidance counselor at the school be involved in his occupational exploration. Working in conjunction with the school counselor will enable the pastor to be better equipped to examine the student's academic record, his capacity to do college work, the nature of his high school courses of study, the indications of interest manifested at school, how he gets along with his peers, and indications of his emotional stability, especially in relation to his peers. These ways of knowing the ministerial candidate are crucial to any evaluation of his capacity to fulfill the occupational requirements of the pastoral ministry. In addition, the school guidance counselor may be in a position to assist the church counselor in facilitating the candidate's growth in self-understanding. In the situation where the potential candidate may not be able to meet the intellectual, social, or emotional requirements of the ordained ministry, the cooperation of counselors from both the school and church will be helpful in the necessary counseling and guidance of such persons to seek another type of occupation.

In addition to the church counselor's guidance involved directly with the individual, and the contact with the school guidance counselor, there should be some contact with the family of a high school student. In most cases, the contact with the parents should be made at a time when both the parents and the young person are present. Areas that may be discussed with the family are the reasons for the interest of the young person, some discussion of the feelings of the parents about this interest, a frank evaluation of the requirements of church occupations, including what is involved in preparation for this work, and sharing with the family ways in which the young person may be enabled to grow in understanding of himself and the commitment which is required of a person preparing for the church-directed ministry.

In all these relationships established for the purpose of the guidance of the young person, an openness to occupational questions and to religious doubt should prevail. Doubts and questions need to be faced honestly in order that a decision may be made on a firm basis. It may be helpful for the pastor to be sensitive to the fact that such a candidate may need to be free from some leadership responsibilities in the church, such as leading a junior high group, in order that he might be a participant with his peers in an ongoing learning situation. He will need to be free to examine all the doubts that he encounters in his academic work. If the church provides the structure in which a high school or college student may continue to examine doubts about his faith and questions about his occupational goals, he will be enabled to mature in his occupational planning, and in some instances his decision to change occupational goals may reflect a mature decision. The continuation of personal relationships with the pastor, who is able to be both firm at some times and permissive at others, will be helpful to the ministerial candidate who is continuing to grow in his understanding of his world, of himself, and of the church and the faith that it proclaims. Such a pastoral relationship may enable the ministerial candidate to mature in his understanding both of his ministry and of the mission of the church to the world.

X

The Fulfillment of Ministry

THE FULFILLMENT OF ANY MINISTRY is, in the last analysis,
dependent upon God's grace. In a sermon of 1521, Martin
Luther had noted that the church might ordain persons, but
only the Holy Spirit could make true ministers of the gospel.
If God did not do it, the ministry of the church would not be
fulfilled.

In terms of the ministerial candidate himself, the fulfillment
of ministry involves more than the achievement of any particular role expectations or self-realization. Any such fulfillment is dependent upon the faithfulness of the candidate and
of the people of God whom he serves. Jesus Christ calls a
person to ministry, and his ministry is ordered by the church.
A candidate fulfills a particular function by the way he exer-
cises his "gifts" (*charisma*), which have been given to him by
God, but it is the grace of God and the faithfulness of the
candidate to his total vocation as a disciple that constitute the
fulfillment of ministry.

Dimensions of Fulfillment

The ministerial candidate's sense of fulfillment in vocation
involves the exercise of his "gifts" (*charisma*) in meeting the
requirements of the church-directed ministry and the actualizing of his selfhood. It means the expression of self through life
and work. The "gifts" for a particular ministry are rooted in a

person's selfhood. While there are various occupational requirements of the ministry, they do not so much provide a
pattern of a role as much as guidelines for fulfilling the needs
of the church and the world, and for the actualizing of a person's selfhood. Although the psychological demands are the
same for every minister, each individual encounters these demands in a highly personal manner. Hence, in the selection of
ministerial candidates, the concern of the church is not so
much a matter of the disqualification of some candidates on
the basis of emotional problems as it is a need to help them to
understand their own psychological needs and goals. Their
needs should be understood in a way that their particular
ministry may be fulfilled through response in discipleship
rather than frustrated by attempting to fulfill the demands of
a particular occupation. If an individual is unable to meet the
psychological requirements of the church-directed ministry, it
is important for him to understand himself in relation to these
occupational demands. Counseling or psychotherapy may be
helpful to the individual in understanding himself in relation
to whatever ministry he has to fulfill. Since every Christian has
a ministry, it is important for the ministerial candidate to discover how this unique pastoral ministry can be fulfilled. The
understanding of ministry involves every member of the community of believers in an exploration of himself in relation to
the will of God as he understands it. Understanding himself in
relation to the need in the church and in terms of his particular
"gifts" of ministry may involve a decision to study for the
church-directed ministry. By the same token, a ministerial candidate may discover that his unique ministry would be frustrated rather than fulfilled by preparing himself for the pastoral
ministry. The occupational goal of a ministerial candidate with
serious neurotic needs tends to be unrealistic in terms of the
lack of understanding of his own aptitudes and interests, and
it is important for him to understand his special abilities and
disabilities. These candidates tend to be influenced by values
and concerns unrelated to the demands of the work of the

ministry. The candidate who is able to face the reality of both his strengths and weaknesses is fundamentally open to the affirmation of God's will and of his self-actualization. Any self-coercive subduing of the reality of his own limitations, in order to prepare himself for the church-directed ministry, will only end in disaster both for himself and for the community of believers. He needs to be free from the kind of self-coercion that subdues reality within himself, and free to be open to the recognition and affirmation of God's grace in relation to the neighbor.

Although everyone seems to want to have a life that is meaningful, there is a noticeable difference between the ministerial candidate who appears to be able to meet the emotional demands of the ministry and those who are not. The candidate who is able to meet the psychological requirements is the very one who is more able to achieve some fulfillment. The less able candidate tends to be primarily concerned with the immediate goals of happiness, comfort, or security, rather than with an experience of fulfillment. He "anticipates" negative reality, and in his fear, he tends to settle for the meaningfulness of security or comfort. The candidate who is better able to meet the psychological requirements of the church-directed ministry "anticipates" a positive reality. Hence, he is sufficiently free from fear so that he can encounter life with courage.

The able ministerial candidate is aware of both his goals and his self-actualizing needs. Such a candidate's sense of fulfillment in vocation involves the exercise of his "gifts" (charisma) and the actualizing of his selfhood. It means the expression of himself through his life and work. The gifts for this ministry are rooted in his selfhood. While there are various psychological requirements of the church-directed ministry, they do not so much provide the pattern of a role as guidelines for the actualizing of his selfhood through the exercise of his gifts. He experiences a sense of fulfillment and actualization through the meaningfulness of the work that involves meeting the need of the neighbor as an expression of obedience to God.

The able ministerial candidate is also aware of the goals that he sets for his life which have implications for the actualization of the self. Man is oriented toward the goal of potential meaning and values that may be actualized through him. Fulfillment of ministry through self-actualization is not the result of a self-realization that simply proceeds from self-understanding. The actualization of selfhood is derived from the commitments that are meaningful to the individual as he responds both to himself and to others. It is commitment to particular decisions that results in fulfillment. Such commitment involves the whole person and embodies what a man judges to be really important. It is not what a man claims as his commitment, but what he shows through his decisions. It is faithfulness to his basic commitments that culminates in authentic fulfillment for the ministerial candidate who is, at the same time, able to meet the occupational requirements of this ministry.

It is the able candidate who reflects this openness to, and acceptance of, both his needs of self-actualization and of the needs of the neighbor. This ministerial candidate anticipates a positive reality and is sufficiently free from fear to be able to experience life more expansively. He is more able to respond both to his needs for self-actualization and fulfillment, and to the broader needs in the world incarnate in the neighbor.

The problem of neurotic needs of ministerial candidates, in terms of their occupational choices, needs to be studied by churches within the Protestant tradition. In the evaluation and counseling of ministerial candidates, there should be a recognition that they need a combination of individual and group counseling, which will treat both the psychodynamics of personality and the explication of the occupational requirements of the ministry. These students will need to understand the dimensions of strengths and weaknesses of their own personalities in relation to the work of the church-directed ministry. Psychological testing and counseling of candidates should not have as its *primary* goal the screening out of psychiatric cases, but of evaluating the significance of any knowledge about the person that may have a bearing upon the future health of his ministry. This primary focus of the testing program does not involve ignoring emotional problems, but it does indicate an emphasis upon the counseling of the ministerial candidate so that he may be enabled to face his own problems and limitations in terms of the psychological requirements of this ministry.

As the result of counseling, the candidate who has made his original occupational choice in terms of real or neurotic guilt may change his occupational goal because of the clarification achieved. On the other hand, the motivation may change so that the needs may become functionally autonomous. As the result of his understanding of the dynamics of guilt, for instance, he may understand the reality of forgiveness and reconciliation in a way that is impossible to comprehend except through experience. At any rate, the institutional church should never add another ordained minister to its roll when this would endanger the future health of a person's total ministry within the community of believers. The ministerial candidates themselves will benefit from the kind of counseling that is primarily concerned with self-discovery and self-actualization in relation to the particular work of the ordained ministry.

All persons seem to want to feel that the goal of their lives has been meaningful. Some sense of fulfillment of meaning is crucial to people. Such fulfillment is contextual in the sense that it is both *intra* and *inter* personal. It involves both the nature of one's interior life, and of one's relationship with the world. To the Christian disciple, this fulfillment involves the discipline of worship and study within the community of believers in which he rehearses the meaning of his existence. It involves the discipline of relationship with people through whom he shows his relationship with God.

Fulfillment Through Self-definition

Fulfillment of ministry may be described by the ministerial candidate himself in terms of his self-definition. It should be helpful for the church to understand fulfillment from this per-

spective. The self-definition of the ministerial candidate involves more than outlining certain occupational requirements,
and it continues throughout his entire life. Both Biblical faith
and contemporary psychology insist that one becomes a real
person only in relationship. Since a person is known only in
dialogue, he cannot know who he really is until he is told who
he is. The ministerial candidate is involved in the process of
learning his identity in relationship with persons who are tell-
ing him who he is. He begins to be defined by the socioeconomic class in which he was born.

The social and emotional stability of his parents will influence greatly his response to faith and trust. As an infant
and child, he may learn the meaning of worship through the
touch of the parent's hand or through the tone of voice. The
degree to which he was held securely and spoken to gently
may influence the degree to which he is sensitive to the meaning of worship. He is beginning to be defined as one who can
respond to trust and to worship.

The degree to which the candidate is disciplined consistently
and lovingly will influence the extent to which he will know
the meaning of self-discipline and self-respect. Knowing himself as finite, he will be better able to judge what he can and
cannot do. He will be free from the tyranny of "ought," and
more free to do what he is able to do. He will need to learn
that discipline and self-control are necessary requisites to any
achievement, but that it is important that such discipline be
used flexibly and not rigidly or compulsively.

His freedom to identify with his father and relate to his
mother will define him as a person who accepts his masculine
role, and yet is free from the role limitations imposed by the
culture. The ministerial candidate may accept his masculinity
without having to prove it to himself or others, and yet he may
be open to the feminine side of his nature in the expression of
his values, interests, and attitudes.

The candidate's home religious environment will define the
values and loyalties that are important to the persons influen-

tial in his life. When religious beliefs are expressed through the practice of his parents, the candidate is defined as a person who belongs to a particular community. When the history of these people of God becomes his own history, he becomes a person who is both "in Christ" and in vocation.

The candidate continues to be defined by his curricular and extracurricular interests, and by his attitudes toward his courses and his academic achievement. He continues in this self-definition in his theological education at an accelerated pace. He becomes academically and vocationally involved in the most deeply personal and existential questions that a man can ever face. He studies about sin, doubt, faith, guilt, and salvation. These questions involve the candidate in a wrestling with his own predicament, that is, unless he keeps them at a distance. He may keep these subjects strictly within an academic discipline as a defense against becoming aware of himself. However, if he insists on relegating these subjects strictly to an academic treatment, the contrast between the academic atmosphere and the highly subjective motivations that were involved in his original "call" to vocation usually results in disillusionment and change in his occupational goal, or in a passive capitulation to role expectations of others. These other persons may be either his pastor, someone on the theological faculty, or any member of the community of believers. His three years in seminary may simply sharpen his technical abilities in theology or his manipulative ability with persons without any development of ethical or spiritual dimensions to his selfhood.

Where a ministerial candidate has considered his choice of the church-directed ministry as a "higher calling" than any other work, he will probably be subject to feelings of guilt and unworthiness. If he is sensitive at all, he will become aware that he is not living up to his own legalistic and moralistic expectations of himself, and he will define himself as unworthy of the office of the ministry. He will either tend toward compartmentalized self-righteousness, or a punishing hostility directed against both himself and members of the congregation. Defining himself as guilty and unworthy, he will tend to project the same sense of unworthiness upon the people of God whom he is called to serve.

The ministerial candidate may also be defining himself as uncertain about his identity. Current anxiety about the church-directed ministry reflects some of the uneasiness shared by other occupations and professions in the cultural crisis of our time. Nevertheless, this anxiety is bound to influence the ministerial candidate. He will need to discover his identity in his particular occupation both by the way he is known by God and his fellowmen and by the work he does. We know ourselves partly through what we do. Vocation is a call to action, and the work of ministry is one of self-definition.

This self-definition also comes through the community of God's people. It is not a man's definition of himself. The people of God define him as he struggles with God's purposes in their midst. This self-definition is not a matter of the members of the congregation forcing the candidate into a preconceived role. Self-definition comes through obedience to God, and through the struggle with his purposes. Self-definition comes from God; but it is communicated through the people of God. Obedience to God is the response to the need of persons. It is the neighbor in his need who proclaims Jesus Christ to him, and who defines him as a person "in Christ."

As he takes up his work, the ministerial candidate will learn that the people of God not only demand his maximum strength, but they will also seek out his greatest weakness. Through his struggles with God's purposes within the community of believers, the candidate will need to be "told" about his weaknesses as well as his strengths. He will be defined as limited. If he allows this work of self-definition to proceed, he will learn to accept his limitations as well as his capabilities. If he refuses to listen to the community, he will try to live by the "oughts" and "shoulds" of an idealized self. He will attempt to have a meaningful life by not being himself. Such glorification of self substitutes the egocentric self-righteousness of a false self for the confrontation with his actual self. It becomes not self-definition but self-deception.

Accepting his definition as finite and limited involves the ministerial candidate in identification with the neighbor at a level of depth that he may not have experienced yet. Sharing his finitude with the neighbor involves his participation in common humanity. Such confession of himself to another involves identification, acceptance or forgiveness, and reconciliation.

All this business of self-definition sounds as if the ministerial candidate is always looking at himself, but he is not working at this definition all by himself. He is being defined by the community of the people of God. Nor is he like a plant that is always being pulled up to see how it is growing and developing. He is not a plant. He is a person, and his roots are always showing. The only question is whether or not he will attempt to hide his roots behind the defensive masks of pious "oughts" or subtle intellectualizations. Some types of counseling or psychotherapy may provide both the basis for discarding outdated defenses and the means for growth in self-understanding.

Fulfillment of Ministry

Fulfillment of ministry comes through the integration that is experienced by the ministerial candidate as he identifies with the image of the true Man, Jesus Christ. This identification involves commitment. Such commitment provides the basis for authentic selfhood in the actualization of the potentialities of the person and for the fulfillment of his purpose in ministry. From the perspective of Biblical faith, man's purpose is fulfilled in response to God's call. If he does not live in obedience to this call, he does not fulfill his destiny, and like a promise that is not kept, his selfhood remains unfulfilled.

We close at the point where we began this chapter. In the final analysis, my fulfillment of ministry is dependent solely upon God's grace. If God does not make true ministers, the ministry of the church is not fulfilled. However, both the work of God and the service of man are involved in the fulfillment of ministry. Within the Protestant tradition, the work of the Holy Spirit and the service of man are not opposed to each other. Rather, man's existence is fulfilled as he responds to God's call, and it is his work, which has been awakened by the Holy Spirit, that culminates in fulfillment of ministry both within the church and within the world.

Notes

1. Geddes MacGregor, *Corpus Christi: The Nature of the Church According to the Reformed Tradition* (The Westminster Press, 1959), pp. 215–216.

2. Robert Clyde Johnson, in *Theology Today*, Vol. XVII, No. 3 (October, 1960), p. 276.

3. H. Richard Niebuhr in collaboration with Daniel Day Williams and James H. Gustafson, *The Purpose of the Church and Its Ministry: Reflections on the Aims of Theological Education* (Harper & Brothers, 1956), p. 64.

4. G. Ernest Wright, *The Rule of God: Essays in Biblical Theology* (Doubleday & Company, Inc., 1960), p. 100.

5. E. F. Scott, *The Epistles of Paul to the Colossians, to Philemon and to the Ephesians* (The Moffatt New Testament Commentary) (Harper & Brothers, 1930), p. 210.

6. *Calvin: Institutes of the Christian Religion*, ed. by John T. McNeill; tr. and indexed by Ford Lewis Battles (The Library of Christian Classics, Vol. XXI) (The Westminster Press, 1960), IV. iii. 1.

7. *Ibid.*, IV. iii. 3.

8. MacGregor, *op cit.*, p. 57.

9. Quoted in Hugh Thomson Kerr, Jr., ed., *A Compend of Luther's Theology* (The Westminster Press, 1943), p. 137.

10. Calvin, *Institutes*, IV. iii. 10.

11. Quoted in Kerr, ed., *op. cit.*, pp. 137–138.

12. *Ibid.*, p. 137.

13. *Ibid.*, p. 129.

14. *Ibid.*, p. 130.

15. Calvin, *Institutes*, IV. iii. 12.

16. *Ibid.*, IV. iii. 11.

17. *Ibid.*

18. *Ibid.*, IV. iii. 12.

19. *Ibid.*

20. *Ibid.*, IV. iii. 14.

21. *Ibid.*, IV. iii. 15.

22. Wilhelm Pauck, "The Ministry in the Time of the Continental Reformation," in H. Richard Niebuhr and Daniel Day Williams, eds., *The Ministry in Historical Perspectives* (Harper & Brothers, 1956), pp. 139–140.

23. Sidney E. Mead, "The Rise of the Evangelical Conception of the Ministry in America (1607–1850)," in Niebuhr and Williams, eds., p. 231.

24. *Ibid.*

25. MacGregor, *op cit.*, p. 80.

26. Robert S. Michaelsen, "The Protestant Ministry in America: 1850 to the Present," in Niebuhr and Williams, eds., p. 271.

27. Niebuhr, *op. cit.*, pp. 64–65.

28. Quoted in Gustaf Wingren, *Luther on Vocation*, tr. by Carl C. Rasmussen (Muhlenberg Press, 1957), pp. 128–129.

29. Donald W. MacKinnon, "The Nature and Nurture of Creative Talent," *American Psychologist*, Vol. 17, No. 7 (July, 1962), p. 494.

30. Charlotte Buhler, *Values in Psychotherapy* (The Free Press of Glencoe, 1962), pp. 104–105.

31. H. Richard Niebuhr, Daniel Day Williams, and James G. Gustafson, *The Advancement of Theological Education* (Harper & Brothers, 1957), pp. 146–147.

32. George C. Stern, "Assessing Theological Student Personality Structure," *Journal of Pastoral Care*, Vol. VIII, No. 2 (1954), pp. 76–83.

33. MacKinnon, *op cit.*

34. Buhler, *op cit.*, p. 96.

35. Karen Horney, *Our Inner Conflicts* (W. W. Norton & Company, Inc., 1945), p. 98.

36. *Ibid.*, p. 109.

37. Glenn E. Whitlock, "The Choice of the Ministry as an Active or Passive Decision," *Pastoral Psychology*, Vol. 12, No. 112 (March, 1961), pp. 47–53.

38. *Theology Today*, Vol. XVIII, No. 3 (October, 1961), p. 357.

Bibliography

BOOKS

Barry, F. R., *Vocation and Ministry*. London: James Nisbet & Co., Ltd., 1958.

Bridston, Keith R., and Culver, Dwight W., *Pre-Seminary Education*. Augsburg Publishing House, 1965.

———— (eds.), *The Making of Ministers: Essays on Clergy Training Today*. Augsburg Publishing House, 1964.

Bromiley, G. W., *Christian Ministry*. Wm. B. Eerdmans Publishing Company, 1959.

Buhler, Charlotte, *Values in Psychotherapy*. The Free Press of Glencoe, 1962.

Calvin, John, *Institutes of the Christian Religion*, ed. by John T. McNeill; tr. and indexed by Ford Lewis Battles. (The Library of Christian Classics, Vol. XXI.) The Westminster Press, 1960.

Coburn, John B., *Minister: Man-in-the-Middle*. The Macmillan Company, 1963.

Davies, Horton, *A Mirror of the Ministry in Modern Novels*. Oxford University Press, 1959.

Farmer, Herbert H., *The Servant of the Word*. Charles Scribner's Sons, 1942.

Forrester, W. R., *Christian Vocation: Studies in Faith and Work*. Charles Scribner's Sons, 1953.

French, Roderick S., *Don't Miss Your Calling*. The Seabury Press, Inc., 1959.

Goodykoontz, Harry G., *The Minister in the Reformed Tradition*. John Knox Press, 1963.

Gresham, Perry Epler, *Disciplines of the High Calling*. The Bethany Press, 1954.

Grimes, Howard, *Realms of Our Calling*. Friendship Press, 1965.

Heiges, Donald R., *The Christian's Calling*. Muhlenberg Press, 1958.

Horney, Karen, *Our Inner Conflicts*. W. W. Norton & Company, Inc., 1945.

Jenkins, Daniel, *The Protestant Ministry*. Doubleday & Company, Inc., 1958.

Johnson, Robert Clyde (ed.) *The Church and Its Changing Ministry*. Office of the General Assembly, The United Presbyterian Church in the U.S.A., 1961.

Kemp, Charles F., *The Pastor and Vocational Counseling*. The Bethany Press, 1961.

Kerr, Hugh Thomson, Jr. (ed.), *A Compend of Luther's Theology*. The Westminster Press, 1943.

Kraemer, Hendrik, *A Theology of the Laity*. The Westminster Press, 1959.

Line, John, *The Doctrine of the Christian Ministry*. London: Butterworth & Co. (Publishers), Ltd., 1959.

McCabe, Joseph E., *Challenging Careers in the Church*. McGraw-Hill Book Company, Inc., 1966.

MacGregor, Geddes, *Corpus Christi: The Nature of the Church According to the Reformed Tradition*. The Westminster Press, 1959.

McNeill, John T., *A History of the Cure of Souls*. Harper & Brothers, 1951.

Manson, Thomas W., *Ministry and Priesthood: Christ's and Ours: Two Lectures*. John Knox Press, 1959.

Moore, William J., *New Testament Concept of the Ministry*. The Bethany Press, 1956.

Niebuhr, Helmut Richard, and Williams, Daniel Day (eds.), *The Ministry in Historical Perspectives*. Harper & Brothers, 1956.

Niebuhr, Helmut Richard, Williams, Daniel Day, and Gustafson, James M., *The Advancement of Theological Education: The Summary Report of a Mid-Century Study*. Harper & Brothers, 1957.

————, *The Purpose of the Church and Its Ministry: Reflections on the Aims of Theological Education*. Harper & Brothers, 1956.

Niles, Daniel T., *The Preacher's Calling to Be Servant*. Harper & Brothers, 1959.

Reid, J. K. S., *The Biblical Doctrine of the Ministry*. Scottish Journal of Theology Occasional Papers, No. 4. London: Oliver & Boyd, Ltd., 1955.

Richardson, Alan, *The Biblical Doctrine of Work*. Alec R. Allenson, Inc., 1954.

Rodenmayer, Robert N., *We Have This Ministry*. Harper & Brothers, 1959.

Scott, E. F., *The Epistles of Paul to the Colossians, to Philemon and to the Ephesians*. (The Moffatt New Testament Commentary.) Harper & Brothers, 1930.

Smart, James D., *The Rebirth of Ministry: A Study of the Biblical Character of the Church's Ministry*. The Westminster Press, 1960.

Smith, Elwyn A., *The Presbyterian Ministry in American Culture: A Study in Changing Concepts, 1700–1900*. The Westminster Press, 1962.

Southard, Samuel, *Counseling for Church Vocations*. The Broadman Press, 1957.

Sweet, Herman J., *The Multiple Staff in the Local Church*. The Westminster Press, 1963.

Wagoner, Walter D., *Bachelor of Divinity*. Association Press, 1963.

Williams, Daniel Day, *The Minister and the Care of Souls*. Harper & Row, Publishers, 1961.

Wingren, Gustaf, *Luther on Vocation*, tr. by Carl C. Rasmussen. Muhlenberg Press, 1957.

Wright, G. Ernest, *The Rule of God: Essays in Biblical Theology*. Doubleday & Company, Inc., 1960.

OTHER RESOURCES

The Church and Every Man's Calling. Division of Vocation, Board of Christian Education, The United Presbyterian Church in the U.S.A., 1966.
This handbook is for local congregations and Christian education committees.

Counseling for Church Related Occupations, Richard H. Bauer, ed. Interboard Committee on Christian Vocations, The Methodist Church, 1964.

Evaluating and Counseling Prospective Church Workers, by Clifford E. Davis. Board of Christian Education, The United Presbyterian Church in the U.S.A., 1966.
This guide describes procedures used for evaluating and counseling registrants and candidates for the gospel ministry and other church occupations of The United Presbyterian Church in the U.S.A. Two supplements that deal with specific tests are available for the use of professionally trained counselors.

Guidance for Church Vocations, by Charles F. Kemp. Department
  of Church Development and Evangelism, The United Christian
  Missionary Society, Missions Building, Indianapolis, Ind. 46207.
  A brief manual on counseling for church vocations that should be
helpful for the adviser of youth.

International Journal of Religious Education, May, 1965. Department of Ministry, National Council of the Churches of Christ,
  475 Riverside Drive, New York, N.Y. 10027.
  This special issue, entitled "Vocation and Church Occupations,"
has helpful articles on these topics.

Vocation and Church Careers Packet. Department of Ministry,
  National Council of the Churches of Christ.
  This packet contains four separate publications on vocation and
church occupations issued by the Department of Ministry. It is
designed particularly for the use of counselors in public high schools.

You and Your Lifework: A Christian Choice for Youth. Science
  Research Associates, Inc., 1963.
  This workbook is an excellent educational instrument on the
meaning of vocation, the choice of an occupation, and church
occupations. It is written for the ninth and tenth grades. A parents'
guide and also a leader's guide, which includes the student's workbook and the parents' guide, are available.